Congratulation, HACE 40th Anniversary!

Since 1982, HACE has been a resource for Latinos, a great partner for companies and a strong voice for Latino's rights. Thank you, HACE, for your relentless commitment to providing access to professional development, career advancement resources, mentorship, and creating a committed network of talented Latino leaders.

I want to dedicate this special edition to HACE's 40th anniversary. Thank you for helping pave the way for the next generation of Latino Leaders. And the next generation of Latino leaders, on your shoulders, lays the responsibility of building a better and more inclusive world.

Marlene González, Author & Executive Coach

LEADERSHIP WIZARD

THE NINE DIMENSIONS; UNLOCK THE LEADER IN YOU. THE DISCIPLINE OF COACHING YOURSELF TO FEARLESSLY LEAD, INFLUENCE, INSPIRE AND EMPOWER OTHERS

MARLENE GONZALEZ

LIFE COACHING GROUP LLC

CONTENTS

Join Our Community 7

Introduction 11

1. LEADERSHIP 17
   What Is Leadership? 20
   Leadership Styles Explained 24
   Why Transformational Leadership? 30
   A Case for Transformational Leadership 32
   Are Leaders Born or Made? 36

2. VISION 40
   Building Trust and Certainty 50
   Being an Intentional Leader 55
   The Fear of Leading Change 63

3. COMMUNICATION 70
   The Qualities of Persuasive 71
   Communication
   Contexts of Effective Communication 81
   Persuasive Body Language 90

4. INFLUENCE 96
   The Nine Soft Tactics of Influencing 98
   Assessing the Effectiveness of Your 103
   Approach

5. ADVERSITY 108
   Coping with Tough Times 112
   Dealing with Mistakes 117
   Conflict Management and Problem 121
   Solving

6. INSPIRATION   130
Understanding What Motivates People   131
Inspire Through Empathy   144
How to Apply Empathy in the Workplace   148

7. COMMITMENT   151
The Role Modeling Wizard   152
Emotions are Contagious   155
Addressing the Factors That Drive Inner Motivators   159

8. EMPOWERMENT   165
How to Delegate Tasks and Build Leaders?   166
A Wizard Encourages Teamwork   170
Take Risks Alongside Your Team   173
A True Wizard Shows Compassion   178

9. DISCIPLINE   188
People Are Habitual Creatures.   189
Discipline Leads to Success   202
What Does Self-Discipline Look Like In Real Life?   206
Self-Discipline Begins With Knowing Your Purpose   213
The Three Traps of Leadership   224

Conclusion   227
About the Author   233
Also by Marlene Gonzalez   235
References   237

This book is dedicated to every person of any race or age who dreams of unlocking the leader in him or her. The next generation of leaders – on your shoulders lays the responsibility to build a better world.

This book is dedicated to my husband, Carlos – you are my rock and thought partner. Thanks for your love and support. My sister, Vanessa, for her unconditional support in making my dream to write this series of coaching eBooks possible.

This book is also dedicated to HACE as well as alumni, mentors, clients and my nieces and nephews. I would like to give you an additional edge, as some of you are just starting your professional journey. To my publishing team – Nick, Myra, Kevin, Susan, Fahi, Dwinny, AIA Team and Publishing Life Services – you are awesome.

JOIN OUR COMMUNITY

Please, don't make the journey alone.

In order to maximize your investment in this book, I encourage you to join our support community on our website www.marlenegonzalez.com.

It is a support group where to share and learn leadership experience and valuable content. We often host free book/audiobook giveaways and helpful resources that will be key to your leadership journey.

It will be great to connect with you there,

Your coach, Marlene Gonzalez

"A true leader has the confidence to stand alone, the courage to make tough decisions and the compassion to listen to the needs of others. He does not set out to be a leader but becomes one by the equality of his actions and the integrity of his intent."

— *DOUGLAS MACARTHUR*

INTRODUCTION

I titled this book series *Wizard* for a reason. As a child, I dreamed of what it would be like to live a life of magic and mystery. You have probably heard the story of Merlin, the wise man of King Arthur's court who started his life as an orphan but ended up becoming one of the greatest wizards of all time. He was known for his great prophetic insight, as well as the ability to control the elements, read people's hearts and alter the perception of reality.

Merlin was also instrumental in mentoring young King Arthur towards establishing a kingdom ruled with kindness and justice. He was also popular amongst the people because he was always eager to share his wisdom and give back to the community. He taught many aspiring wizards to achieve their greatness, never afraid of being surpassed by his protégés.

If there were ever a true grass-to-grace story that attests to the fact that bold leadership could attain great feats, it would be the story of a little black girl from the southern state of Mississippi. Transformational leaders like Oprah Winfrey serve to transform the lives of the people they meet for the better. Their decisions are rooted in the premise that the most important thing is how others are impacted. The question for them is always "How do I do the most good? How can I elevate others? How best can I empower those who follow me to be their best selves?".

The fact that Winfrey has handled her success with grace despite her childhood is astounding. To add to that, she has touched many people's lives with her impudence, wit and kindness. Her charismatic leadership style is known to draw people close and rally them behind her. She never fails to inspire people with her thoughts. She has influenced many with her stature and her presence.

This is not a book about Oprah Winfrey, though, as impressive as she is. This is a book about you. Like Merlin, Oprah, and people like me, must overcome the tremendous challenges that come our way to achieve leadership and power in our society. It is about people who must harness their weaknesses and play to their strengths to lead and influence others. It is about true leaders whose boldness of vision and faith in what the future could bring is infectious.

Oprah is often referred as the "queen" of all media. In the game of chess, the pawn goes first and it is the most critical piece and the only piece that can transform itself into an influential figure. The pawn transforms into another piece of the player's choice: a queen, rook, bishop or knight of the same color. Usually, the queen is the chosen one, and a promotion is often called queening the pawn.

In the game of leadership, you must check all the boxes, learn to play the game, outsmart other players, and prove yourself worthy of leadership positions. New leaders face similar challenges like feeling voiceless and invisible, lacking proper representation, role models, mentoring or sponsorship opportunities.

Every person has the power to be a leader. That power is within you. The responsibility to awake the leader that lies within you is yours. It would be best if you claimed that power. The ability to lead is unique to you, and it is not about titles or positions. It is about finding your voice as a leader. Do you envision a leadership role for yourself? Do you need to get out of your comfort zone? Do you see yourself as a leader? You sense that you were destined for greatness. But it does not comes as naturally to you as breathing. You need a little more confidence and training to embrace your inner leader.

Perhaps your dilemma is not that your reality differs from your potential. You are already in a position of some influence. On good days, things go well, and people follow you gladly. The good days are few and far spaced, though. You have trouble gaining the trust and respect of the people you are leading. When you think you have crossed a hurdle, something else comes up and erases all the progress you had made. You wonder what you could do differently.

Let me make a radical statement here: to be a great leader, you must unlock the magic that comes from within. This is what this book is about – understanding what transformational leadership is and then exploring its nine dimensions and facets to unlock your leadership potential.

You will explore the different dimensions and assess what type of leader you want to be. What do you bring naturally to leadership? How do you adapt your leadership style in different contexts? What do you need to do to unlock your potential? Which dimension do you find easy and which do you find difficult? Lastly, what legacy will you leave as a leader?

This book will describe the aspects of transformational leadership and use the term "transformational" as less about the style of leadership and more about helping to transform you. As such, you will understand why empathy is important in leadership and explore strategies to develop discipline, continuous motivation and a committed team.

When I first took on a leadership position, I had a lot of respect for teams and from team members. I was knowledgeable about the project and adopted a hands-on work ethic that helped when interacting with my team. I was sure that whatever came at me, I could handle it. I soon learned that these were just table stakes. The qualities gave me the opportunity, but I was not really prepared for leading a large team. I had a lot of training, but none of it covered leadership. Most of my training was concerned with managing people, projects, planning, documenting and implementing plans. I had to learn through many mistakes.

In my work, I partner with organizations and leaders to inspire people and transform teams to meet common leadership challenges and find their leadership voice. I have held many executive corporate positions in the United States, Europe and Latin America and currently serve on many boards and non-profit organizations. I am the former Senior Director of Global Training,

Learning, and Development for the McDonald's Corporation.

For me, coaching is a beautiful, collaborative process between the coach and client, in this case, you, the reader. You are the main character. I will share the nine dimensions that I use in my private coaching practice. This book is not a textbook about leadership. It is about coaching you to unlock the magic of leadership within you and successfully lead, inspire and help others grow. Stay engaged, read on, reflect on the different topics, commit to applying and adopting a new leadership behavior and journal your way through it.

You can read the entire book from beginning to end or go straight to the dimension you feel drawn to the most.

The journey is yours to take. Let's begin!

1

LEADERSHIP

Historically, a few personalities have stood out in distinct fields during different time periods. There have continually been individuals who stand out to lead an entire population. In the 1150s, there was Frederick Barbarossa, the King of Germany and the Holy Roman Empire's emperor. Barbarossa was named King of Germany in 1152 and later obtained the Roman emperor's identity from Pope Adrian IV. His identity, Barbarossa, means "pink beard." During his reign, Barbarossa sought to restore the empire to its lost glory by connecting Italy and Germany.

Alexander the Great is another famous name. He is remembered as an army commander who was never defeated in battle throughout the 15 years he ruled. Before his death, Alexander ruled an impressive empire stretching from Pakistan to Greece. Think of others like Julius Caesar, Winston Churchill, Cleopatra and Mahatma Gandhi. Gandhi was born an ordinary boy. However, he had a dedication to excel at everything he did. After completing his studies, he became part of the Indian freedom warfare in opposition to colonial rule. Gandhi had a non-violence policy, protesting through civil disobedience. He is remembered for his people skills, resilience, knowledge and motivational approach to leadership.

The remarkable stories of these trailblazers mark the books of history. We celebrate these men and women for going from adversity to the extraordinary and how they redefined influence. Yet, the age of influential people has not come to an end. Even today, there are still those who stand out in and by the things they do. Bill Gates is an entrepreneur and philanthropist who has inspired a whole generation of innovators. Very few people have done for their industries what Gates has done for information technology.

Gates saw his first computer when he was 13 years old. He had to pay to use it in school, and when he was out of money, he hacked into the computer to use it freely. Gates grew up in a middle-class family in Seattle and showed a knack for entrepreneurship when he was young. By 15, he had started a business, and five years later, he was on the edge of changing how the world does business. His business strategy and work ethic made Microsoft what we know today, leading to his wealth and philanthropy. By the time he stepped down from Microsoft's leadership, he had made his mark in the world.

Oprah Winfrey's story is another example of a contemporary leader overcoming the odds to empower a whole generation, in her case, of women. She is not just a talk show host. She is one of the most influential business leaders globally with a significant influence on mainstream society and popular culture. She has come a long way from rural Mississippi. Her battles started with horrible sexual abuse in friends' and relatives' hands and ended with what we know her to be . *Forbes* ranked Winfrey as one of the wealthiest African Americans in the 20th century.

So there you have it – many influential people whose stories inspire and visions remain alive even beyond the grave. What is it that made them stand out from the rest of the world? Despite the differences in their backgrounds, times, landscapes, race and gender, what do they have in common? This chapter will give you a comprehensive definition of leadership. Here, you will find a comparison between transformational leadership and other leadership styles to help you see why transformational leadership is your surest bet to achieve more than you ever thought possible. It will introduce you to the nine secret leadership dimensions of transformational leadership that I will explore in detail for the remaining part of the book.

WHAT IS LEADERSHIP?

One of the universally accepted definitions of leadership is the process of creating an inspiring vision for the future. However, this definition fails to define the paths and mindsets that great leaders followed. It disregards the unique feature great leaders have in common and the ideas that made them great. To get a better definition of leadership, it is vital to understand what leadership is not.

Leadership is not about seniority or one's position in a company's hierarchy. It has nothing to do with titles or even personal attributes. Leadership is not even synonymous with management. One of the biggest lies people have bought into regarding leadership is that leadership and management are the same. Do you have 10 people in your P&L responsibility? Good for you! Hopefully you manage them well because good management is needed. Managers need to plan, monitor, measure, hire, fire, coordinate and look after many other things. Yet, managers typically manage things, and leaders lead people.

Leadership is not about saying the right thing or ordering other people around. Of course, it will involve telling people what they need to do, but the best way to do that is by helping them see what they need to do on their own. Leadership is about coaching and mentorship, not controlling and micromanaging. It is about doing the right thing and not just being a mouthpiece for truth. Leadership is not about knowing what should be done or making the decisions. It is not learned in the classroom but is mastered from falling on your face, brushing the dirt off and trying again. You cannot achieve leadership by reading books. It is neither about your ego nor never failing.

Leadership requires personal influence and persuasion afforded by a long track record of strong relationships built on trust. Leadership is not power. Writing a traffic ticket, dismissing someone from a team or hiring or firing someone does not make you a leader. Stopping buyers from entering your store or collecting on an overdue book does not confer the leader's title on you. People in these positions could show leadership, but leadership is not inherent in their positions.

Leadership is also not about pride. Have you ever wondered why the most successful people never stop learning, reflecting, growing and adapting to do better in their businesses? The less successful and poor leaders often lean back as if they have nothing new to learn. Leadership is not about doing everything that needs doing yourself. It is not about doing all the communication necessary, although leaders need to be great communicators. Leadership is not about always feeling confident and having all the answers. It is not demeaning others, taking credit for all the work or deflecting personal responsibility.

The late Peter Drucker, an Australian management consultant, defined a leader as someone with followers. Everyone with a Facebook account would be a leader if that were true. Imagine an army captain with a team of 200 soldiers who never leaves his room. He issues commands and the soldiers obey because they have to. Is that captain a leader? Bill Gates defines a leader as anyone who empowers others, but as close as he is to the actual definition, it still falls short. You have to empower others towards an end. Leadership expert John Maxwell said that leadership is influence, but a kidnapper demanding ransom has influence. Are they a leader? The concept of leadership draws a lot of attention. It has many definitions, but few of them cover it well.

If leadership is not all those things, what does it become?

Leadership is a process of social influence that maximizes other people's efforts towards achieving a specific goal.

If you break down this definition, leadership is comprised of the following key elements:

- Leadership starts from social influence, not power or authority.
- Leadership requires other people. They do not need to report to you directly.
- Leadership includes a goal. It is not just an influence, the outcome of which is undefined.

Notice how this definition does not mention the leader's attributes, personality traits or even their title. What causes this definition to be different is that it includes maximization of other people's efforts. A person could use their influence to organize others, but a leader must maximize the effort. Effective leadership should also include trust built by transparency, openness, competence, consistency, direct and clear communication, concern and compassion, and a positive attitude. When people observe these things in the leader, influence compels them to listen and accept the leader's opinions and ideas as their own.

LEADERSHIP STYLES EXPLAINED

The more the world has evolved, the more the styles for leadership have changed. People have come up with new leadership style theories, and those have been added to the list now and then. By taking time to familiarize yourself with each of these leadership styles, you will recognize the areas where they are lacking and will be able to compare them to see the best style.

1. Autocratic Leadership Style

This style of leadership is leader-centered. The leader carries all the authority, instructs his subordinates on what to do, when to do it and how. He supervises his team closely, expecting the subordinates to obey. The autocratic leader drives results through authority, fear of punishment or other negative rewards. This style offers quick decision-making, allows a centralized working system and has a strong motivation for the leader because they dictate the terms.

The fundamental problem with this leadership style is that subordinates do not know why they perform a specific task. They have to blindly follow the leader's directions which may cause them to feel helpless and frustrated. Since the employee is not consulted, success relies entirely on how efficient the leader is. This style cannot assure the continuity of an organization and subordinates do not get a chance to develop, meaning that this style works only for the short term and in projects that require speed.

2. *Laissez-faire* or "Hands-off'" Leadership Style

Here, the leader gives his subordinates all the power to act as they will. He defines the limitations and goals for an action and then leaves the subordinates to do the rest. The leader, for the most part, makes contact with outsiders to bring information to the group. Subordinates enjoy the freedom to make choices and be creative in problem-solving.

The problem with this style is that sometimes team members do not know their role within the group. This also means a lack of accountability since no one has a specific task and it encourages passivity among employees. After all, why should you do something you do not have to?

3. Democratic Leadership Style

Under democratic leadership, team members participate in decision-making. Each member can share their opinion, experience and knowledge about a project. When feedback has been factored in, the leader makes a choice. This style allows members to share new ideas openly. It is a style anyone can practice because you can consider different perspectives and evaluate possible outcomes before choosing. Team members feel that their voice matters and are more willing to participate in problem-solving. Relationships built in the system are team-based because loyalty is essential. Honesty is a priority for the democratic style to work. Since members work with the big picture, they have a higher level of job satisfaction.

The downside to democratic leadership is that if misapplied, it can cause disharmony. Think of a leader who consistently chooses one person's opinions over the rest of the team. Leaders could also begin deferring decisions to the team. What happens if the team never reaches a consensus? This means that there will always be a struggle to define leadership because everyone is equal. The outcome is not always positive.

4. Transactional Leadership Style

Transactional leadership is based on rewards and punishment as the motivators for employees to drive results. The system is rigid, and the process is predefined so that if you achieve the requirements, you get the reward. Otherwise, you get punished. If well implemented, transactional leadership creates a sense of fairness. Feedback is fair since it is based on metrics rather than the manager's feelings and opinions. The process could even be automated using human resources-type software. Transactional leadership is easy to understand because it is structured, and employees can see what impact they have on the business.

The problem with this style is that rewards do not work for everyone. Transactional leaders are not strong on building relationships. They do not focus on the working conditions, which works against the business in the long term. The business is further strained because it is difficult to find the right rewards to motivate all employees. You end up stifling creativity and performance. Since transactional leadership focuses on rewards and punishment, the goals tend to be short-term. Leaders do not look at the big picture and do not develop employees to step up when there is a vacant position.

As businesses have used these styles, it has become clear that some things need to change. For example, flexibility is necessary for leadership. It is important to have a style that marries well with your organizational culture and benefits your business. Over time, leaders realized that they do not have to stick with one style of leadership. They combined styles to meet different business teams and functions. Soon enough, other styles of leadership came up. Some of the recent leadership styles that have had better success than the previous ones include:

5. The Visionary Leadership Style

Visionary leaders can drive progress and pave the way towards change by earning trust and inspiring their employees to try new ideas. They can establish strong organizational bonds and foster confidence among colleagues and direct reports. The visionary style of leadership works well for small, fast-growing organizations or businesses that are restructuring. The leader tends to be strategic, inspirational, optimistic, innovative, bold and persistent – traits that unite teams, help companies grow and improve outdated practices or technologies.

However, visionary leaders may miss important details because their focus is on the big picture. They find it easy to sacrifice the resolution of present problems because they dwell on the future, leaving the team feeling unheard.

6. Servant Leadership Style

Servant leaders have a people-first mindset. They believe that when team members feel professionally and personally fulfilled, they are more effective. Due to this emphasis on collaboration and employee satisfaction, servant leaders achieve higher respect levels. Servant leaders are skilled in building team morale and helping people to re-engage with work. They boost employee loyalty and productivity, cultivate trust, inspire better decision-making and create future leaders.

However, servant leaders can burn out easily because they put the needs of their teams before their own. They might have difficulties being authoritative when necessary in the service of organizational goals.

7. Transformational Leadership Style

Transformational leadership is the focus of the rest of this book. It is a style similar to that of a coaching leadership style that creates a high-performance culture characterized by collaboration, empowerment and fulfillment. However, the leader does not place a majority of their focus on each employee's individual goals. The commitment to the objectives of the organization drives the transformational leader. The transformational leader spends a lot of their time on the big picture, meaning that employees have leeway to work without constant supervision. Transformational leaders provide encouragement to their teams, are creative, inspire others to achieve their objectives and place a high value on challenging their teams. They value personal connections with their team members, which boosts retention and morale. They value the company's ethics and those of the team.

WHY TRANSFORMATIONAL LEADERSHIP?

Renowned leadership expert, James McGregor Burns first introduced the concept of transformational leadership. According to Burns, this style includes a leader and followers who push each other to become morally better. Through their personality and vision, the transformational leader inspires their followers to change their expectations, motivations and perceptions as they work toward a common goal. Another researcher later expanded the concept of transformational leadership to include the leadership's impact on its followers.

Have you ever been in a tough situation and watched someone take control? Did you observe them passionately communicate a vision for the group in a way that made everyone else feel energized? If you have, you saw what a transformational leader looks like in action. These leaders are not just involved and concerned about the process, but they also look to helping each group member succeed. They stimulate team members to achieve extraordinary outcomes, and in the process, grow in their leadership capacity. Transformational leadership is inspirational leadership.

Inspirational leadership goes beyond the definition of leadership. Earlier in this book, we said that leadership is the process of social influence that maximizes others' efforts towards achieving a goal. Inspirational leadership does not just influence others. It appeals to the team members' inner motivators to create a commitment to change and action. The result is team members who are empowered to act.

Note that inspirational leadership is not a state of "being." It is a set of behaviors. Action is inevitably tied to leadership. For example, a leader could be optimistic, but being optimistic is not a behavior. An inspirational leader will give others a positive and engaging vision of the future. Similarly, being a role model, however admirable, is not an action. Role modeling is a form of inspirational leadership, but it works only if the leader models good values that matter to their team members. Empowerment is not about inviting other people to participate, say, in a discussion. It requires action on the part of the "empowered."

Transformational leadership will go a long way in addressing behaviors that stem from other people's true "inner motivators," values and emotions. To practice inspirational leadership, the leader must appeal to their team members' values, touch their emotions or do both together. Inspirational leadership will not just energize your followers; it should also cause them to be committed to action. To do this, the leader must set targets, make people accountable, delegate and offer feedback.

A CASE FOR TRANSFORMATIONAL LEADERSHIP

The world has seen many forms of tragedy – genocides, wars, killings, riots and famines. While some tragedies, like famines, may have little human influence behind them, others, like genocides, have been driven by men of influence. There are men in history who advocated crime to levels no one else could imagine. Adolf Hitler is one such man. He was the *führer*, a ruthless and tyrannical leader of the Nazi Party and the Chancellor of Germany. The creative and brutal dictator was mainly responsible for World War II and the Holocaust. He believed that Jews were the cause of all problems and he wanted to eliminate them. His actions claimed over 50 million lives.

Joseph Stalin was a Soviet Union dictator for 31 years. Before that, he was a robber and an assassin. Terror and violence characterized his reign, and his decisions caused a famine that claimed millions of lives. Stalin even killed the families of people who loved him. Vlad the Impaler reigned as prince from 1448 to 1462 in

Wallachia. He had a sadistic personality and is said to have killed nearly 20% of the population. He once impaled a victim through his buttocks until the stake came out from his mouth. Vlad is said to have roasted children and fed them to their mothers. He would cut off women's breasts, fed them to their husbands and then impaled them.

These men are some of the many examples in the history of power wielders. Many other people throughout history led others, but they were destructive and inhumane. Do we still consider them to be leaders? What is it that separates a power wielder from a leader?

To answer this, we have to go back to the definition of a transformational leader. The difference between a power wielder and a leader is the moral aspect behind the pursuit of their goals. The ends do not ever justify the means for a good leader. A good leader chooses right because it is right and pursues their goals within the limits of what they know to be ethical. They focus on the means of achieving their goals more than they focus on the outcome. The point here is that you should never follow a leader blindly. Leaders are not always the people who step in to save the day. Like the rest of humanity, they are human, and have both good and evil in them. Stay away from the person with influence whose intentions are evil. They can wreak havoc in ways you may not imagine. If nothing else, learn from history.

Both good and bad people can gain influence, sometimes with a lot of skill. Yet, the measure of true leadership is not just the ability to influence. Hitler was not a leader despite the many people who followed him. Stalin was not one either. As I have made clear before, leadership's success is inspiring people towards a worthwhile goal, affirming their humanity and their gifts to collaborate towards certain objectives.

Other than the definitions, though, two other things need tackling before we can dig deeper into transformational leadership. The internet is filled with a lot of research on why good leadership increases revenues for an organization. People agree that the impact of good leadership is unparalleled. Human instinct to naturally follow the good leader further testifies the importance of leadership, which makes one wonder: why are there still so many bad leaders? Is there something we can do about it or are good leaders born with it?

To answer that question, we have to consider two things: our perception and reality. First, we know what leaders look like, but we are confused about what constitutes a good leader. Our confusion incapacitates us from working to become good leaders. We do not consistently support and require leaders to be great, which means there is no motivation to improve. The second issue is majorly affected by the first. If we do not know what makes a good leader, how can we push someone to become one? Besides, in businesses, senior executives often allow their organization's leaders to get away with being mediocre. A good leader gets excellent results consistently while building a capable and committed team. If leaders still keep their jobs without getting great results, why should everyone else in the organization think that that is okay? Without any real consequence to mediocrity, nothing will change.

To improve your organization's leadership standard, you have to know what makes a good leader and then structure everything else, from hiring to promotions, around that. You have to celebrate people who demonstrate such leadership and fire those who don't. The good thing is that leaders have changed for good. You would have had to deal with problems 10 years ago that are not even an issue now. For example, while there are still some authoritarian and autocratic leaders, they are no longer the norm. Today, leaders are expected to listen to their followers and respond to their needs. They are expected to mentor, coach, support, develop, empower and care for their team members.

Embracing transformational leadership will solve these problems for you for good. Transformational leaders are valued all over the world. Authentic transformational leadership affects all organizations and cultures because the goals of the transformational leader transcend self-interests. The leader works towards the good of the organization. Transformational leaders are unique because:

- They have influence and charisma coupled with a high standard of excellence.
- They are inspiring and motivational.
- They are compassionate and considerate.
- They challenge their followers to think for themselves and think critically.

ARE LEADERS BORN OR MADE?

Whether leaders are made or born has been a subject of debate among specialists for a long time. People have wondered if some have it in their genes to attain glory in life or if becoming a successful leader is acquired over time. Researchers have tackled the question, examined the evidence and some are convinced that leadership is primarily inherent. Research supports this conclusion. Researchers compared 1,795 results from people who filled a personality test at 16 years old and then again 50 years later. They looked at 10 facets of personality and zoomed in on leadership. The idea was that if leadership is inherent, then the personality test results would be consistent 50 years later. Otherwise, there would be a sizable increase in leadership in the five decades.

To assess leadership, participants had to indicate how much they agreed with statements like "I am influential," "I love making choices" and so forth. 79% of the participants had the same results across 50 years. They had the same opinion of themselves at 66 as they had when they were 16. 17% had a reported increase in leadership while the rest had a decrease. Held independently, these numbers may not say much, but they take a different meaning compared to other personality dimensions. Of the dimensions tested in the research, leadership was most likely to stay consistent throughout a person's life. Traits like calmness, self-confidence and tidiness had a similarity of less than 55% in the five decades. The researchers found leadership to be the most resilient to change. This study suggests that those who argue that leaders are born could be right.

The other side of the argument has experts who are convinced that leaders are mostly made. The best research estimates that leadership is about 33% innate and 66% made. Leading a military unit, country or organization, and doing it well, is a complicated task. To expect someone to be born with everything they need to do the job does not align with what is known about the complexity of social processes and groups – which means that the notion that leaders are mostly made is suitable for anyone who would be involved in leadership development – that way, the leaders can be developed. Of course, some genetic characteristics predispose some people to leadership.

Research points to extraversion being associated with leadership. Some evidence points to risk-taking, boldness and assertiveness being an advantage for leaders. They typically have to think through situations and find the right course of action, which lends to the suspicions that intelligence also has a role to play in leadership – more specifically, social intelligence. Along with social intelligence in leadership, there is a need to be empathic enough to know your followers. The leader should know what their followers want, when and what is in the way of their getting it.

One wonders, though, whether that means that people who lack those characteristics are disqualified. Are introverts ruled out of becoming effective leaders? What about those whose social intelligence is average at best? Would non-empathic people make for terrible leaders? There are many people interested in leadership development who lack the correct answers to these questions. They are constantly tossed to and fro, never quite settling it in their hearts whether leaders are made or born. Of course, if you never settle this question, there is only so far you can go and so much you can do towards becoming a better leader.

The best resolution for the tension between research on this topic lies in transformational leadership. Earlier in this book, it was mentioned that transformational leadership is a set of behaviors. It is not a state of existence. The leader does so through behaviors and actions. In defining the inspirational leader as one who regularly behaves a particular way, inspirational leadership becomes a skill you can learn. It becomes something that anyone can master with conscious and intentional actions and through continued practice.

2

VISION

Theodore Hesburgh, the former president of the University of Notre Dame, once said that the essence of leadership is a vision well-articulated on every occasion. He was spot on. Few things are as demoralizing as leaders who cannot articulate why they are doing what they are doing. Good business leaders must own their vision to drive it to fulfillment. They must share the direction and dream that other people can share and target, and the vision must be more than a written vision and mission statement. It must permeate the workplace and be seen in the organization's values, beliefs, actions and goals. That way, it affects every employee regardless of their job description.

Leadership is about going somewhere. A vision defines the place. This chapter explores what a vision is, how to create a compelling one and then communicate it to induce your followers' trust and commitment. It talks about implementing a structure of traits, skills and principles aligned with your vision and how to live out your values in a practical way, modeling your ideals to your followers. It empowers you to walk the talk and become a leader others can trust.

A wizard and warrior leader has a vision. They can see the present plainly and imaginatively invent a future that others can work to accomplish. The visionary leader does not live in the future, though. They are firmly grounded in the present, yet convinced that they could forge a better future. In this sense, a vision is an end that a leader sees and directs his resources and energy towards. The leader shares a dream and path that employees understand and are compelled to follow. The vision acts as an internal propelling force for the leader and then the followers. It powers the leader to move forward despite different obstacles and unites the team with a mutual goal.

Without a vision, work has no meaning. Employees clock in and do their hours out of duty. They spend their workdays counting down to the month's end when they receive their salary and do other things they find more interesting. A vision provides direction. It serves as a guidepost for averting catastrophe before it appears. It is the vision that allows employees to determine what would be valuable for the business and what to avoid. It helps employees to feel connected to something larger than themselves and each other.

A vision is more than a statement pasted on all company brochures and marketing paraphernalia. This begs the question, "What makes for a powerful vision?". The vision must be:

Oriented towards the Future

By its very definition, a vision lives in the future. It is a mental picture of what could be – a goal that everyone can work towards. In a world that rewards an ability to be in the present and solve current problems, a vision must look forward. What will your team look like a year from now? What about in five years? That way, you can orient everyone toward that future.

Context Creating

If a vision is so far into the future that it appears impractical to the team, it is not a strong vision. A good vision must be relevant for your team. It must have context so that it can create shared meaning for other people. For example, if you run a bookstore to equip students with relevant material, your vision might include empowering students with knowledge. You could tie this to statistics that show the need for quality study materials in the internet age. In other words, your team must know how their work matters and how it will play out in the future. Do not assume that your followers can make it out for themselves. It is more preferable to be redundant than to have an ignorant team.

Clear, Credible and Motivating

Your vision cannot just be a statement with famous words that hardly mean much. A good vision must set the direction of the business and its purpose. It must do so in a way that inspires loyalty and stimulates all employees, encouraging them to get involved. It must be so atomized as to display and reflect the organization's strengths, beliefs, values and culture. That way employees can believe that they are genuinely part of something larger than themselves.

Positive

No one wants to work towards a dark future. A vision needs to speak to possibilities without fixating on problems. The visionary leader sees problems as a challenge to overcome and communicates that with infectious enthusiasm. A vision that points in an inspiring direction will inspire enthusiasm, excitement, belief and commitment.

Concrete, Challenging and Inclusive

People easily believe their efforts to be inconsequential, assuming that they are just one cog in the wheel. A visionary leader helps everyone in their team connect to the larger objectives of the business. The leader challenges others to improve themselves by communicating inclusive visions. In the communication of these visions, everyone plays a meaningful and vital role. The vision is regularly shared and communicated in monthly reminders, announcements and via other communication methods at every organizational level.

Active, Rational and Innovative

A visionary leader keeps their vision alive through action. It is pointless to have a vision that you never reference. If you become bored talking about your vision, it needs to be tuned up. For the employee, the vision should be the reason for choosing a course of action. As the leader, you hire, develop products and select markets based on your vision. The vision challenges employees to stretch themselves and innovate. Embed your vision in every step of interaction with the business.

Now that you know you need a vision to make a difference and what makes a powerful vision, you are likely wondering how you would go about shaping your business's vision. To have a healthy enterprise, you must build alignment across the business's leadership and broader organization. Without alignment, everyone at work will be committed to something, but it is unlikely to be the same thing. Minor differences between players can cause confusion and diffuse effort, slowing your pace. It takes a well-shaped vision to help people work together despite their differences – to stay aligned. As such, it will take you time, effort and a rigorous and honest approach, but the benefits of a compelling vision are worth it.

There can be numerous starting points to vision shaping, but the key initiative is to answer the question, "Why do we exist?". Without this, you can lose your sense of direction. Everything is allowed in because you have no boundaries. The answer does not have to be unique, but it has to be authentic, real and genuine. This is why vision-shaping starts with you. Look inside yourself and draw on your desires and natural gifts. Look at your calling if you know what it is. Consider how you want your life to be remembered. How do you want to contribute to the broader world? What would your life be about if it was well-lived? Answering these questions will strengthen your vision muscle.

Secondly, revisit your history. Your vision must not be detached from your past. If you talk to any successful leader, you will discover important events in their past that instrumentally contributed to their vision. While looking at past events, repeat and deepen the questions you ask yourself. If you have identified an event, ask yourself why it is important. Follow your responses with another question to uncover what lies underneath your answers. The insights and realizations will help you eliminate some things and keep others.

Lastly, your vision must meet other people's needs. A true vision goes beyond what any one person can do. If it has value, a vision does not just include other people; it adds value to them. Think about how you want to serve others and how they would benefit from your service. You can think about the different stakeholders in your life separately – community, family, workplace, friends, partner and so forth. How might each want to receive your service and how would you do it?

When you have cleared these things up, you can translate this approach and your answers to your organization. What is important there? Explore the impact it has had and the possibilities for why it exists. Find out which one of them inspires the most. As you do this, consider the impact you want to have on your community, suppliers, customers, shareholders and employees. Each of these considerations will awaken a possible reason for your existence. Zero in on what is the most important.

With your vision at hand, you are a step closer to being a wizard and warrior leader. Now it needs execution. Executing a vision may be one of the most challenging competencies you need to develop. The three components necessary for the success of a vision in its execution include:

Defining and Communicating the Vision

You must define your definition clearly, even if you are not sure how you get there. It ensures your team can identify where you are at any one point and how close you are to your goal. The destination should be exciting even for your team. Buy-in begins with a clear and exciting vision, but it is sustained through communication – how you live and celebrate that vision. Not only do people need to understand your vision, but they also need to be reminded and shown what it looks like to be personally invested in it.

Strategic Thinking

Your strategy defines the way you achieve your leadership vision based on some external and internal factors. It is the route to your goal. The strategy makes sure you are ready for anything that may happen in the market. As a pro-tip, use visualization to develop strategic thinking.

A Visualization Exercise

Carve out some time and find a quiet place. Think back to one of your fondest memories. Where were you? Who was with you? Add to the mental picture as many details about your surroundings as you can – sights, smells, sounds and so forth. Do you remember how you felt during the memory? That is the clarity necessary to create a future you can look forward to. What do you hear, see, feel and experience? Ensure that your vision is as straightforward as it would be if it had already happened.

Note that strategic thinking does not have to be a solo activity. You can bring in people you trust to offer different perspectives and views about your business. They might identify assumptions you have made from confirmation bias.

Plans and Priorities

Vision and strategy without a plan will only cause frustration and burnout. You end up investing energy without focus and wasting time. The lack of focus, structure and follow-through means that no one takes responsibility for the great ideas in the vision. A well-executed vision must have a plan. Your team can identify key wins and know where to pour their expertise and energy.

BUILDING TRUST AND CERTAINTY

Digital platforms like social media and search engines have become major news gateways in today's world. Algorithms are used to highlight news and ads consistent with the consumer's preferences. This networked environment has caused uncertainty about online information, which has impacted the way news is received globally. Now more than ever, perceptions of trust in news found on search engines and social media are lower than traditional news media. That is not the only way trust has been impacted. For example, it is difficult to distinguish an actual photo from one that has been airbrushed and edited for clout. Advertising language has made it so that people can hardly believe what they see. Internet hoaxes make things worse, coupled with occasional news of the greed of some organizational leaders. Trust is a hard commodity to get nowadays.

All this is happening alongside the struggles of many global economies. There is low job satisfaction globally, and engagement with trustworthiness is identified as one of the necessary qualities for a leader. Employees, though, are not the only ones with trust issues. Leaders also struggle to find employees they can trust, but that is a subject for another conversation. Reduced trust always affects relationships, organizational bottom lines, the goal of a business and well-being. One often finds themselves wondering how to begin building trust in a time of cynicism and distrust.

One thing is clear: if people hear your vision, respect it and work with you to achieve it, they must trust you. Your team needs to not only trust your leadership but also each other. How do you earn that trust? If you have lost it, how do you earn it back? For starters, trust has three cornerstones:

1. A Right Definition

Often, what people imagine trust to be trust, it is not. If you misunderstand what trust is, you set yourself up for unfulfilled expectations and broken promises. Even though people mean different things by the word "trust," it is primarily about authenticity.

2. Authenticity as the Builder for Trust

Only authentic trust will build relationships that last, and that trust is built when the parties involved are committed to it. The relationship has to be more important than any outcome, and reciprocity must be central in any exchange. The parties have to deliver on their mutual commitments without being primarily concerned about their gain and without attempts to manipulate.

3. Trust Starting with Trust

People generally talk about trust as something you get, and yet trust is earned. You get trust because you give it. In this sense, trust is something you do. You choose to trust someone. Trust starts with trust the same way respect starts by respecting others.

The world today may be discouraging when it comes to trust, but there is hope. Research has found that a small act, like collaborating with someone or being generous instead of selfish, can make a difference. The effective leader must be courageous enough to go against the grain. They understand that workplace trust is necessary if the people are to thrive, and they work to create that trust. Influential leaders grow authentic trust at work in the following ways:

- **They excel at their job.** At work, competence takes the day. It is a building block for performance trust.
- **They love their work.** Here, love is more than cheerleading or forced enthusiasm. It is an inner drive that comes from a desire to see their vision achieved. For many effective leaders, it is about being the change they want to see. It is subtle in some leaders and pronounced in others, but it is always there.
- **They are always self-aware.** Effective leaders are mindful of what they say and do. They operate with behavioral integrity and self-alignment. They do not make commitments that they cannot honor and never delegate responsibility for their mistakes.
- **They care about others.** Effective leaders work with compassion. They see others as individuals, not through stereotypical, generational or gender biases.
- **They pursue what is best for others.** Effective leaders inspire others to be their best selves. They encourage and develop their gifts, providing opportunities and challenges to help you be where you desire. They work to make more resources available for everyone and to

create an environment where everyone they lead is successful.

- **They listen.** They are not always thinking of what they will say next. They listen to understand and learn. They are adept at withholding judgment and engaging in genuine conversation that facilitates connection.
- **They have perspective.** Effective leaders never lose sight of the things that truly matter. When they find themselves in the middle of a work crisis, they do not yell at their employees or fire them at the first sign of trouble. They think about things before making serious decisions. They look for context, knowing that sometimes things simply do not work out no matter how hard you try.
- **They manage work, not people.** Effective leaders help people understand their vision and what it looks like to meet it. They set the direction without nit-picking on the details. They get rid of challenges and bureaucracy to make it easier for people to do their job.
- **They are quick to express gratitude.** Effective leaders appreciate value. They acknowledge their followers' efforts and contributions towards a task.
- **They see past themselves.** Effective leaders are

not just concerned with getting a bonus, promotion or hitting a specific milestone. They see the big picture. They understand why they do their job and help others inject meaning into their tasks. They are the reason their employees see what matters.

Simply put, effective leaders have many ways to grow trust. They know that they cannot attract the best ideas, talent and contributions without trust. Effective leaders are intentional.

BEING AN INTENTIONAL LEADER

Without intentionality, others will find it difficult to understand and believe in your goals enough to make your vision a reality. In leadership, intentionality is about a sustained focus on an initiative or a goal. The goal has to have meaning and purpose for the business. Whenever people interact with the intentional leader, they view him as deliberate. He has a clear plan that everybody understands. They know what they are doing and why.

Think about the last time you came up with a plan. Where is the plan now? Chances are that it has been gathering dust on the shelf because you developed it with your mind and not your heart. The plan has no soul. It was simply something you did, enjoyed the high of creating it and then moved to the next thing. The end goal was to finish the task rather than releasing the spirit. You did it the same way that most people live their lives – based on assumptions. You forgot to account for how you have changed and to question those assumptions. The goal of intentionality is to step away from those assumptions into more concrete thinking, and this must be the foundation of everything in your business. To run your business with intentionality:

1. Understand That a Business Is Driven by Its Leadership

The leadership in your organization should be intentional. Intentionality can be defined as examining yourself to find out how you would prefer things to run before making that the reality. Most leaders who are competent stumble upon competence. Few have intentionally molded their leadership. Instead, their leadership is guided by the way their life plays out. Since they cannot describe their leadership, they are often inconsistent in their practice. No wonder every member of your leadership needs a leadership agenda.

2. Create a Story for Your Organization

Employees typically have four types of needs, and most companies meet only three. They have physical needs, which means they want a good salary and working environment with good benefits. They have mental needs that translate to a desire to grow in the workplace, develop new skills and find challenging work. They also have emotional needs which have to do with recognition and reward. Most businesses meet these three needs adequately but hardly ever touch on the spiritual need. Their work does not feed the spirit.

You may argue that your business exists to make money, but that does not provide a long-lasting incentive. While companies do need to make a profit, their purpose cannot be to profit-make. Purpose has to feed the spirit. Companies that have figured this out give their employees the power to innovate. Here, your company story is the reason for your existence – your purpose in the world. Why will the world be better because of you? An intentional leadership should drive this.

3. Create a Unified Intentional Brand and Culture

A brand is the way outsiders see a business. It is the perception that customers have of your business, while culture is the view from inside. It is how your employees see your business. The two are related and need to be unified. Before the social media age, companies could be intentional with their brand by conducting CSR and public relations campaigns, among other efforts. With social media, people have a more intimate view of business operations. The safest avenue is to have your culture reflect your brand. Work on the culture with intentionality and use those foundations to create the brand.

4. Build an Intentional Strategy

When you have your culture and brand driving your strategy and the business's story fueling it, your strategy has heart. It can inspire. It can appeal to the hearts of your employees, and you can define your leadership as intentional.

As a leader, you must not just have your business built on the foundations of intentionality; you must also embody the trait. An intentional leader is not just a decisive or assertive leader. They are focused on a goal. Research points to the need for more intentionality in leadership. Otherwise, you have slow strategic execution for your plans that wastes talent and money. Employees tend to get discouraged and lose their drive, often stopping projects they started well.

Intentionality is not autocratic. It does not suggest a ruthless abiding by a plan. Intentional leaders know when to be flexible in their execution. They are aware of things as they play out in real-time and encourage their followers to keep on moving. In a meeting, for example, an intentional leader will let people discuss. They will clarify when they are giving a recommendation or when they have made a choice. They will encourage people to speak up and compliment those who do. They close the meeting with deadlines and accountability, which leads us to your mission.

A mission is a pragmatic statement of what you have to do every day to move closer to your business vision. A mission differs from a vision. A vision describes your future position. A mission defines your business, its objectives and its approach to get to those objectives. It is your mission that puts intention in your vision.

Have you ever wondered why some brands seem to do better than others? People just keep coming back to them. For those businesses, price and convenience may play a role in drawing customers, but the primary reason people return is because they have found a connection. Those businesses demonstrate a purpose that people have no difficulties supporting, and that is the power of a well-written mission statement. A mission statement is an action-oriented statement explaining the purpose of your company. It provides a summary of what your business does – its products or services, goals, employees, owners and core functionality. It explains what you do and why. Depending on the type of business, your mission statement could even explain your role in the world at large.

While some people use "mission statement" and "vision statement" interchangeably, they are different. Your mission statement provides a roadmap for achieving your vision statement. Your vision statement guides your business aspirations. It is important to note that your mission statement could change over time as the business grows. It is okay to make adjustments when necessary. As a rule of thumb, write a mission statement only when you want to add clarity to your business's vision for the sake of your stakeholders. Writing it should be an opportunity to define business goals, norms, ethics and culture, and not to tick it off a to-do list. To write a compelling mission statement:

Start by Defining Your Market

A good market definition explains what the need is and who the target customer is. It talks about the way your business differs from others and clarifies what the business does not do. Imagine working with a real person who wants your service or product. Why do they want it? How did they come to know about your business? Make the story as concrete as you can and maintain that even when writing the actual statement. If you have trouble beginning, you can start by making a list of what your business does and does not do.

Define the Service or Product That Your Business Offers

Begin writing your mission statement by clarifying the work you do. Use your market story to identify what makes your business special for the customer you are targeting. Be careful not to undervalue your business. You do not have to be saving the world, but offering a good service, if zoomed into your specialty and location, is excellent. Make sure you write down what is unique about your business. If what you do serves the broader world, include that but make sure it is not a generic statement that could apply to any business.

Explain How Your Business Serves Its Employees

Any good business will be good for its employees, too. Having satisfied employees is better for your productivity than turnover. This is why the culture in business matters. Do you reward employees? How do you motivate them to do better? A mission statement can explain the benefits an employee gets from working there. Do not just assert those benefits; make sure the statement is true.

Qualities such as empowerment, diversity and fairness matter, but since every existing business says it values them, work to have a differentiator to make your goals more concrete. Do not concern yourself so much about uniqueness at this point because some traits here are shared among businesses. If you have a unique view of how you interact with employees, like offering remote workplaces, state that in the mission. It is not always that you must focus on employees, but it is a good practice.

State How the Business Benefits Its Owners

It is alright to have things like enhancing the stock value as one of the things the business offers its owners, but that will likely be generic. You would be wise to add whatever else gives you an edge. For some people, it is creating a business that others are happy to work in, which could be added to their mission statement. Many mission statements tend to be aimed at the customer alone, so they hardly mention the benefit to owners. When you incorporate it, you set yourself apart.

Discuss, Edit, Clean up, Review and Revise

A good mission statement will serve many functions, define business objectives and be functional for the long term, so this step is necessary. You can develop a complete mission statement for use within the organization, and then create a subset for the public. Many companies segment their mission statements and categorize segments by goal or type. Make sure the mission works for your business. As you edit, remove any general terms and buzzwords. If it does not explicitly apply to what you do, it needs to go. Phrases like "world-class" or "excellent customer service" do not mean much because they are all over the place.

You can read mission statements from other companies, but make sure yours describes your company. If you do not believe what you have, no one else will. Ensure that there are no half-truths in the statement. You can show your drafts to others and factor in their opinions without arguing. Edit until you have something worthwhile. As the business evolves, review and revise the statement to reflect changes in the business.

THE FEAR OF LEADING CHANGE

Once you have a vision, it may not be easy to get others to accept and adopt it. Generally, people are resistant to change. This is natural because change is uncomfortable, and it requires new ways of doing things and thinking. People find it difficult to see what their lives will look like if they agree to change, and so they cling to what they know. Employees, however, do not fear change for its own sake. They fear what they do not know. They fear that they could lose control.

Such fear is understandable because change can create uncertainty and anxiety. Employees lose their sense of security. They have no idea how the change will affect them, but only that they will be affected. A good leader knows how to lead change effectively in their workplace. They know that change is essential for the success of any business. Any organization that does not continually change will become obsolete.

Ongoing change drives adaptation and innovation. They recognize that what they expect of the employees plays a role in resistance to change. If you introduce change expecting an outcome set in stone, with either total resistance or no resistance at all, you will be setting yourself up for disappointment. Introduce change with a positive mindset believing that employees want to cooperate. With such a mindset, you can make the best of every situation and support change across time. The idea is to believe the best about your employees.

Secondly, you can make a habit of communicating well. Ideally, every employee would get a chance to join the discussion and provide suggestions for the changes you want to make. Practically, this can only work if your organization is not too large. In a company-wide effort, it might not be easy to get an input from every employee. The overall direction, in that case, would have to come from senior leaders. When it is so, form a leadership team. The team could contain some employees from the organization or senior leaders and managers with oversight on certain parts of the organization.

If you have a communication culture in your workplace, the opportunity for input could reach the soldiers on the frontline. Whether you have input, as the core doers at work, you can reduce employee resistance by:

Owning the Changes

Change can come at any point in your business. Sometimes, it has nothing to do with you. It does not matter where the change started; you must own it because it is your responsibility to implement it. You can only implement change effectively if you believe in it. This may be harder when the change does not begin with you. After you have made sure that the change is inevitable, accept the decision. If the organization has decided to move, fall in line and do what you can to make it happen.

Avoiding Biased Support

Half-invested support undermines everyone else's effort. If you cannot support the change entirely, it may be time to move on. You can do a lot of damage by offering support only when you feel like it.

Communicating the Change

How you communicate the change has the most impact on how much resistance you get. Begin by explaining why it is necessary. Specifically, let employees know what they can or cannot do. Discuss change implementation and how to make it work and answer any questions that might come up. If you have reservations, you can share them but explain that you will offer full support. Ask employees to join you. Emphasize that even though you have the skills, you need their help to move forward. Everyone is critical to make the change work.

Helping Employees to Understand How They Gain from the Change

Some of the resistance will disappear when employees understand how they benefit from the change. Communicate the benefits to the group, organization and different departments but stress the personal impact of the change. This will help employees understand why they should give their time, commitment and energy to change. The idea is to make employees feel compensated for the energy and time they spend.

Listening to Employees

Expectedly, employees will experience different emotions when faced with the necessary change. Never minimize their response even to changes you think are simple. Perhaps the change is trite to many employees, but it makes a significant impact on one employee's task. Hear them out and allow them to share their perspective. That will reduce some of their resistance to change.

Empowering Employees to Contribute

Among the top things that employees want from their jobs is control over their tasks. When trying to reduce resistance to change, you will do well to factor in this aspect. Find ways to allow employees control over some aspects of the change. If you communicated clearly and transparently, they know the rationale, direction, goal and parameters for the organization. Empower them to execute the change in that framework. Delegate whenever you can and have critical path points to receive feedback in place.

Creating a Feedback Loop

You may follow these steps and still have a change that is not optimal. It would be best to keep communication open throughout the business to ensure that feedback reaches the relevant employees. Continuous improvement is expected in any business change. Augment this with a willingness to examine the steps you are taking to ensure you are going in the right direction.

Leading change will demand you to understand and respond to many human emotions. You must also do this continually if you are promoting ongoing change. You can also promote ongoing change by:

- Creating a vision and sharing it often with employees. Be sure to demonstrate your commitment by continuously behaving in a way that will move the organization closer to its ideal.
- Promoting new initiatives that improve the organization.
- Involving people in discussions to improve commitment to change.
- Communicating reasons for decisions made that do not involve frontline employees.
- Removing roadblocks so that when desirable changes seem to be slowing or sputtering out,

you know why. Identify unexpected obstacles and remove them.

- Celebrating initiatives that aim to improve performance, whether they succeed or not.
- Including change and innovation as core competencies. Ensure that you have change agents and that they are promoted into positions of influence.

3

COMMUNICATION

All through history, the best leaders have known how to encourage others to pursue a goal. The ability to motivate was always tied to communication skills. Following the example of historical leaders, today's leaders have to prioritize and hone their communication skills to guide their teams well. Research shows a link between effective leadership and communication. In one study, 44% of the business leaders responded they were unhappy with their employees' work. Out of the group, 70% felt the need to improve their communication to improve motivation and deal with performance issues. About 70% of the managers in the group that was happy with their employees' performance owed their success to communication.

Leadership wizard demands that you know how to persuasively communicate with different people in your organization, from managers and employees to investors and customers. Each of those groups will require a different leadership style and different communication. Leaders have to adapt based on the group they are addressing, but effective communication principles can apply to all situations. Transformative leaders know and value these skills. In this chapter, we explore non-verbal and verbal communication strategies for successful communication.

THE QUALITIES OF PERSUASIVE COMMUNICATION

Persuasive communication will ensure that you are prepared to handle the different types of relationships at an organizational level and sometimes globally. You need to think clearly, express your ideas and share information with many audiences. You have to learn how to handle fast-flowing information in the organization and among partners, influencers, stakeholders and customers. Persuasive communication is composed of the following qualities:

- Clarity. There is no effective communication without simplicity. You cannot afford to be vague when talking with your team. They have to understand the task, how long it is to take, the resources they need and any other information that could make the process easier. Otherwise, productivity will suffer.

- Personalization. Leaders often have to speak to groups. A good leader knows how to make each person in a group feel like they are being addressed individually. The communication skills of the leader make everyone feel important.

- Transparency. The transformative leader knows that he has to communicate transparently for his team to trust him. He cannot afford to have a hidden agenda or to share half-truths because those breed anxiety and distrust.

- Feedback. The best communicators know that sometimes what people hear is different from what was said, and so they check in and verify that they were correctly understood. If they were not, they change their style and try again.

- Constructiveness. Great communicators know the difference between aggressiveness and straightforwardness. They do not point out problems without offering solutions. This helps them avoid sounding pushy and instead provide value to every member of the team.

- Inspiration. Of all the principles of effective communication, inspiration might be the most important. The effective communicator can rally their team around a vision and help them understand, accept the vision and work toward it.

Other things have a role to play in communication too. Tone of voice will have a lot to say on how your message is received, for starters. With other non-verbal cues, your tone will give context to what you are saying or the takeaway from your message. Saying one statement with a sharp tone and an eye roll will be essentially different from making the same statement with a soft voice. The words may be the same, but your presentation makes a difference.

Secondly, as a leader, you must understand why it is important to find common grounds. Compromise can allow you to work optimally. Compromise is about finding a balance that works well for all the people involved. It will sometimes mean that you tailor your approach and be flexible, but it serves to grow your team and makes conversations more fruitful. In this context, compromise is a way to settle differences by mutual concessions. You reach an agreement by adjusting your opposing claims and modifying your demands.

Compromise is not a weakness or strength in leadership; it is a measure of experience and maturity. Leaders who have more experience can better determine when to stand their ground and when to let up a little. The willingness to compromise shows an awareness and commitment to the bigger picture over the need to always be "right." American businessman, Stephen Covey argued that compromise must create synergy. The real leader knows how to resolve issues alongside other people as much as they can.

The first step to effective communication is active listening. Most people do not know how to listen, why they should and how to improve their listening skills. Active listening is critical for effective leadership. Managers who make listening a part of their leadership style make a lot of progress in employee productivity and engagement. Those who lack basic skills to communicate their expectations and provide feedback suffer the consequences.

Being a good listener is not always what people think. It is not just keeping quiet as others speak or only repeating what others say. Those are part of the process, but great listeners do not stop there. They enter every conversation with a sense of curiosity. They listen to understand and focus on things like tone, facial expression and body language. They ask questions that are thought out and prompt the speaker to explain something more. Great listeners have a way of making others feel safe. They convey support and confidence and can spark cooperative conversations. Below are some reasons why you should aim to become better at listening:

Listening helps to build healthy relations in the workplace.

Healthy communication is necessary if you are to achieve and sustain success. Research shows that only 13% of workers in the United States think their organizations' leadership communicates well. Improving how you communicate will set you apart from other players in the business world.

Listening increases employee productivity and engagement.

Different factors contribute to employee engagement, but strong evidence points to the need for listening. Leaders who want employee engagement can begin by listening to their employees' challenges. Whenever you listen and deal with your team members' issues, you support your employees and make their environment better, which is necessary for engagement.

When you listen, you learn from your team members.

Running a business is too complex for one person to deal with it alone. Your team members have knowledge and insight you would be better off knowing. This includes their issues but also touches on the big picture. Your team members will see things that you do not because they know your customers' needs. Listening will allow you to tap into that reservoir of knowledge.

You will encourage innovation and creativity.

Whenever you listen well to your employees, you create room for transformative conversations. You invite a spirit of co-creation and encourage your team members to collaborate in innovation. Listening fosters a creative give-and-take that allows your business to see different angles and possibilities for the future.

By listening, you will stay abreast of the changes in the workplace.

Even before the global pandemic, many leaders had taken to creating remote workplaces. The global workplace was shifting, and organizations were rethinking their structures. Shifts like this can only happen with good listening and communication. It depends on exchanging ideas across functions, teams, cultures, digital platforms and national borders. Only a leader who knows how to listen well can navigate such a complex landscape.

Leadership experts currently think that the most influential leaders can teach their team members. They do this by providing support and encouraging growth. They learn and take risks instead of giving directives and advice. They lead with questions that encourage creative thinking. Listening is at the heart of such a leader. There are three levels of listening. In the first level, the listener gets easily distracted because they are trying to come up with a response instead of focusing on the speaker. In the second level, the listener wants to understand the context of the message, reflecting what they have heard. In level three listening, you are fully attentive, focused and listening with no judgment. You pay attention to voice tone and body language. The effective communicator should use level two and three listening.

You can start honing your listening skills today by learning the techniques involved in active listening:

1. Pay Attention

Look at the speaker as they deliver their message and give them your full attention. If you have distracting thoughts, put them aside and acknowledge what you are hearing without thinking of a response. If you are in a distracting environment, you can find a quieter place to help you listen better. Make sure you pay attention to the speaker's body language.

2. Indicate That You Are Listening

Your gestures and body language need to communicate that you are engaged. Nod often, smile and have an open and interested posture.

3. Offer Feedback

Our assumptions, beliefs and judgments often distort what we hear. The effective listener looks to understand what is being communicated, and this may demand that you ask questions. You can reflect on what is being said and summarize the comments of the speaker.

4. Hold Your Judgment

Interrupting someone as they speak wastes your time and frustrates the speaker. It limits communication. Let the speaker finish expressing themselves before you ask questions and hold your counter-arguments.

5. Respond as Appropriate

In active listening you encourage understanding and respect. In doing so, you gain perspective and new information. You will not get anything from putting the speaker down or attacking them. Be honest and truthful in your response. Explain your opinions with respect and treat the other person how you would want them to treat you.

As a rule of thumb, people who listen well typically:

- Spend less time talking.
- Listen to be influenced rather than to rebut ideas.
- Rarely start their sentences with "but".
- Understand any biases that they have and work consciously to overcome them.
- Ask open-ended questions.
- Take notes to ensure they have all the details.
- Paraphrase often to confirm understanding and show that they have captured the essence of what has been communicated.
- Do not finish other people's sentences.

CONTEXTS OF EFFECTIVE COMMUNICATION

The way you communicate will depend on the context in which the communication is taking place. There is a difference between one-on-one communication, speaking in a group setting and communicating in unexpected moments.

But whatever the context, some things must remain true. For instance, an effective leader will learn how to keep the conversation going and the communication lines open. They are accessible, always maintaining an open-door policy. Always pick the right time to share your ideas and listen to others. This will mean that you are always aware of your role in the conversation. Listen to what others say and end the conversation with clarity. That said, the contexts of communication include:

1. Communicating One-on-one

The greatest mistake that most leaders make is assuming that their employees believe, agree or understand them because they have power and influence. No wonder communication problems happen all the time. The good news is that you can avoid many communication breakdowns with a bit of attention and care.

The point of communicating one-on-one is to give direction, gather information, solve problems, show empathy, make decisions, share ideas and offer encouragement, but some things like noise, perceptions, typecasting and cultural differences can get in the way. When communicating one-on-one, provide feedback. This could mean nodding appropriately or using words like "uh-uh" to encourage the speaker to keep speaking. Pay attention to the meaning of their communication instead of what they are saying. To do that, notice the following:

Eyes

The saying, "the eyes are the windows to the soul", is common because people's eyes can tell as much as their words do. You can use the eyes to gauge intelligence, truthfulness and the feelings of a speaker. Conversely, a failure to make eye contact can have dire consequences. It is not unheard of for lawyers in court to be ordered to avoid eye contact with the juror to avoid swaying them. This is how important eye contact is. Our pupils respond to our emotions and betray different feelings. For example, they dilate when a person is interested, receptive or aroused. It is so important to see a person's eyes in communication that wearing sunglasses is considered rude in some contexts. Studies show that people who make regular eye contact in conversation are considered more trustworthy.

Facial Expressions

The human face is naturally expressive. It can convey many emotions without uttering a word. Facial expressions are universal. The facial expressions for sadness, happiness, fear, surprise, and disgust are the same across cultures. Pay attention to facial expressions in communication.

Voice Modulation

It is not just what people say but how they say it that conveys meaning. In communication, the effective listener can "read" other people's voices in addition to listening to their words. Pay attention to pace, timing, volume, inflection, tone and sounds as they add to the message.

Proximity and Posture

Have you ever felt uncomfortable in a conversation because the other person stood too close? Space is an important aspect of communication. Although this differs depending on the situation, culture and the closeness of the relationship, we all need physical space. When communicating, use physical space to signal affection, dominance, intimacy or aggression. While at it, notice how people sit, walk, stand or hold their heads. A person's posture can provide a lot of information about who they are.

To become a good leader, you have to master body language. Body language is the use of expressions, physical behavior and mannerisms to communicate. It is done instinctively, not consciously. Whether you know it or not, you are giving and receiving wordless signals as you interact with others. Those signals can cause others to relax and help you to build trust or they can offend and undermine the message you are trying to convey.

In some cases, the things you say and what you communicate via body language could be different. If your words speak one thing and your body language communicates something else, your listener will find you dishonest – like saying "yes" while shaking your head. In the face of such mixed signals, the listener has to choose what to believe – the non-verbal message or your verbal one. They will likely choose the non-verbal message. By improving your understanding and use of non-verbal communication, you can connect with others better, express what you mean clearly and build better relationships in the workplace. Non-verbal communication can play the following roles:

- Repetition. It strengthens your message by repeating it.
- Accenting. It could underline your verbal message, as in raising a fist after an inspirational speech to motivate people.
- Contradiction. It can go against what you are trying to communicate, painting you as dishonest.
- Complementing. Non-verbal communication might add to your verbal message. A pat on an employee's back, for example, in addition to

praising them, can increase the impact of your message.

- Substitution. Non-verbal communication can take the place of words.

Body language plays a huge role in leadership communication. When it comes to persuasion, it has to work alongside your voice. Your vocal codes are a muscle in your body, and the way you use them can impact your persuasiveness. Typically, attempts to persuade are either argumentative or non-argumentative. You are non-argumentative if you use body language and other social actions, like buying a meal, in your favor. You can also use rhetoric to persuade. Former United States President, Barack Obama was elected for his rhetoric. As a leader, you can use rhetorical devices to make your language beautiful and to persuade. For the best persuasive skills, use the following vocal techniques:

Emphasis

You can emphasize by repeating words to create continuity, connection and rhythm. You can repeat words in succession, or you can repeat after some intervening words. Repetition can even be carried to the following line to bring out how ideas are connected.

You can repeat groups of words or clauses; the point is to emphasize your main ideas.

Pace

Pace refers to the speed of your speech. Speeches delivered fast, fluently, and loudly are usually more persuasive than those delivered at moderate speeds. Pace helps you to capture and keep attention. Slow your pace down when you want to seem thoughtful and when you want to give the impression that you are thinking through an issue as you speak.

Vocal Fillers

When giving a presentation, fillers can destroy and steal from your credibility. Vocal fillers are things like 'er' and 'um.' To be an effective communicator, you need to eliminate them from your speech.

Pitch

Pitch has to do with the lowness or highness of your voice as you speak. People interpret deeper voices as more authoritative. Both men and women with deeper voices are stereotypically considered more believable. You can practice lowering your voice to enjoy the benefits of a lower pitch.

Volume

You will not be persuasive if your audience is straining to hear what you are saying. Whenever you can, always test your voice before a presentation to make sure everyone can hear you. Conversely, watch against shouting or yelling – it could aggravate your audience.

Articulation

Make sure that you pronounce every phrase, word, and sentence well. Coherent and clear speech communicates competence. On the other hand, sloppy articulation signals laziness or a lack of education, taking away from your credibility.

Pauses

Pauses can be an excellent resource if used properly. A well-timed pause gives others time to catch up with you. It can also help you to relax when you are rattled. Use pauses to drive your point home and to highlight important points.

Sound Repetition

Repeating a sound can produce harmony and subtly link ideas, and emphasize words. There are two primary sound repetition forms. Consonance repeats the same consonant sound, like saying 'dimes get lost daydreaming in dark gutters.' Alliteration repeats the same consonant sound at the beginning of each word, like in 'curiosity killed the cat.'

As you consider these things, remember that rhetoric is not just the logic but the eloquence and beauty of your speech. It also has to do with how vivid you are. Beautiful language easily slips and affects the soul, giving you influence.

2. Communicating with Groups

As you lead your organization, many opportunities to communicate will come your way. You will have to participate in informal interactions as you make casual conversation in the workplace. You will need to lead small meetings and communicate in formal settings. You may also have to make presentations at board meetings and employee information sessions. Whatever the situation, remember that time is money.

Leaders should focus their communication on the crucial things that affect their organization's performance and handle the issues that are important to their people. For example, your employees might want to know the direction of your organization. You may want to share strategies that you will use to achieve success and communicate with your team members to understand their role in achieving your objectives. Leadership will also demand that you provide regular updates to your employees on the organization's progress and commend them when they do well.

Before you hold any meeting where you will be communicating with your people, answer the following questions:

- Who am I meeting, and what do I want to communicate?
- What is the best way to pass my message?
- How do I ensure that I get the biggest bang for my buck in the meeting?
- How do I reduce resistance and pushback?
- How do I respond to concerns and questions that come up?

PERSUASIVE BODY LANGUAGE

Body language is the non-verbal element of communication. So far, we have established how important body language is and how to be more aware of other people's reactions to what you do and say. This section focuses on helping you adjust your body language to appear more approachable, engaging, and positive, increasing your persuasiveness. In understanding body language, you can present yourself better and use your demeanor to enhance what you are communicating verbally.

Research shows that 55% of people form their perceptions about us primarily through body language, 38% through our tone, and only 7% through what we say. This means that as a leader, the way you gesture, speak, and even your facial expressions, will impact your leadership style. Here is a guide to using body language to enhance your message:

Eyes and Face

In interpersonal interaction, eye contact helps to give and receive feedback. Looking at your audience helps you to know whether they are paying attention or seem disinterested. If you avert your eyes too frequently, communication may not be smooth, and if you maintain too much eye contact, you are perceived as trying too hard and dishonest. Eye contact also communicates when someone else may speak. It is typically continuous when you are listening than when you are speaking. Eye contact also communicates about the relationship with your audience.

Like your eyes, your face shows what you feel. These affect displays are often inadvertent, which is why there is a high possibility of them conflicting with your words.

In some cases, as a leader, you will need to manage your emotions so that your face does not betray them. You have to know your 'tells.' In a card game, for example, people who cannot control their facial expressions give away information about their hand, causing them to lose.

Hands

The way you use your hands signals to others what you are feeling. Pocketing your hands or tucking them behind your back may appear like you are holding back. Covering your mouth or your ears as you speak paints a picture of dishonesty. Stroking your chin makes you seem thoughtful, and laying your hands on the table as you speak suggests that you agree with your audience. Even the way you shake hands can make or break your business deals. A firm handshake indicates alliance and cooperation.

Head

If the person you are communicating with tilts their head towards you, it could be that you have them hooked on what you are saying. The opposite is also true. Nodding indicates agreement. When walking into a room, how you hold your head communicates authority or meekness – hold your head high to have a presence.

Legs

If the person you are conversing with has their feet pointed towards you, they are interested. Legs pointed away from the speaker indicate boredom or disinterest. If you cross your legs while standing, it may indicate awkwardness. If you cross them while seated, it shows resistance. Tapping one's foot testifies to boredom unless you are dancing, of course.

Posture and Mannerisms

How you stand communicates how you think about yourself or a situation. Someone pacing about may be nervous. A relaxed posture is tied to openness to communication. Tapping one's fingers communicates impatience. Fidgeting is a sign of boredom and clutching objects tightly conveys anxiety.

Touch

Subconsciously, we liked to be touched, which is why touch can be an important psychological tool. Touch makes people feel loved and appreciated, but there is a need to differentiate between appropriate and inappropriate touch. For example, research shows that women do not like being touched by other women, but they are tolerant to appropriate touch from men. Safe areas to touch include hands, forearms, shoulders, and upper back, depending on the situation and the relationship.

Mirroring

The idea behind mirroring is to match your body image and movements to the other person's demeanor. The goal is not to mimic them but to reflect how they feel. Mimicry creates offense – people do not like to be imitated, but mirroring builds rapport if you do it well. Because your demeanors are similar, your audience feels a sense of connection. They lean into their instinct to accept influence from those they deem to be similar to themselves. You can mirror body language, vocabulary, speech rate, mood, energy level, and even breathing.

As you hone your body language communication, bear in mind that different gestures can mean different things in different contexts. The okay sign is one such gesture. It consists of touching the tips of your index finger and your thumb to form a circle while the other fingers point straight. In the west, this gesture is positive; it means that all is good. In France, it means zero, and in the Middle East, it indicates the evil eye. Another example is the finger snap. In some contexts, it attracts attention, like when you have a good idea or when you just remembered something. In other contexts, it is a rude way of asking someone to hurry up.

It is also important to remember that human communication is summed up by its parts. None the elements discussed in this chapter works on its own. One reason people have trouble communicating on email and social media is that those mediums have no room for non-verbal communication, which results in loss of meaning.

4

INFLUENCE

As the world changes and organizational layers and hierarchies reduce, developing influencing skills has become necessary for today's workplace. You can only achieve success with others. The ability to influence, sometimes without formal authority, is necessary. The leader must draw on who they are and what they do to inspire and engage people. Yet, influence is not just about getting others to agree with you – you may be able to get them to cooperate even when they do not agree.

Influence is also not winning at whatever cost and always getting your way. It is about behaving in a way that invites others to change their thoughts, behavior, attitudes and ways to accommodate your wishes while accepting that they may be unwilling, unprepared or unable to meet your request. This chapter will explore the different social influence approaches and suggest the best influence strategies that transformational leaders use to inspire change.

We defined leadership as an act of social influence. Influence is the primary mechanism through which the leader enacts their leadership. It cannot be divorced from leadership. Mastering the art of influence is necessary for every leader. Successful leaders must learn to use different influence tactics. For example, a manager may want to influence their employees to accept and do new assignments, change their schedules and plans, provide relevant and timely information or discontinue inappropriate behavior, all of which will require a different approach. Note that influence can be with people, events or things and its effectiveness and strength often vary. Research has found nine different influence tactics, which can be categorized as either soft or hard tactics.

Hard tactics leave their target with less freedom than soft tactics. They often threaten the target's autonomy and try to get a result by pushing them in a specific direction. For example, as a leader, referring to your authority when making a request could be considered a hard tactic. Yelling also fits this category. By nature, hard tactics are simple and straightforward. The leader will carry them out by building on their perspective.

On the other hand, soft tactics are influence behaviors that are constructive and thoughtful. They allow the target more latitude in deciding whether to accept the influence. This means that they tend to be more complex, requiring an influence based on the followers' inner motivators, characteristics and perspectives. The result tends to be a committed target as opposed to forced compliance from the target of hard tactics.

THE NINE SOFT TACTICS OF INFLUENCING

1. Requesting

Requesting is the simplest of the hard tactics. The leader makes simple demands of their target to get them to act. Requesting is obtaining a commitment from the target by making a direct statement of what you want and asserting your position clearly and confidently. A typical statement of request would look like:

- *"I would like you to know that ..."*
- *"I asked you to inform him. Have you had a chance to do that?"*
- *"Could you please call Frank and ..."*

2. Legitimating

Legitimating is a bit more complicated than requesting. The leader adds rationalization or legitimation for the command. They seek to establish their request's legitimacy by implying or inferring authority or a principle to issue it. It does not matter whether the invoked authority is implicit or formal as long as it is recognized by the person you influence. Examples of legitimating include:

- *"Our policy dictates that all travel must be ..."*
- *"As you know, it is standard practice to ..."*
- *"The CEO asked me to ..."*

3. Coalition

Coalition resembles legitimating, but its standing does not come from a reference to authority. When a leader uses this approach, they enlist help from other people and use their support to get their followers to do something. For example:

- *"Jake and I think that ..."*
- *"Everybody thinks this to be a good idea."*
- *"Everyone on the finance team says ..."*
- *"As a team, we decided to ..."*

4. Rational Persuasion

In this tactic, the leader uses logical arguments and factual evidence to prove that a request is both feasible and relevant to the critical objectives. They have to make a case for their approach. Typical statements by a leader using rational persuasion include:

- *"I want you to ... The facts suggest three reasons for moving ahead this way ..."*
- *"Given the available data, the most logical approach is ..."*
- *"The company's transformation is necessary to reduce costs, grow and beat the competition."*

5. Ingratiation or Socializing

Socializing typically uses flattery and praise during or before an attempt to influence others towards a particular action. It means establishing a basis for making a request, behaving cordially and warmly to influence other people to act, be friendly, build a relationship or disclose personal information. A leader who is socializing could say things like:

- *"I also have two kids ..."*
- *"I am very impressed by your achievements. They*

show a lot of dedication and commitment. It would
be great if you could ..."

- *"'I see the problem the same way ..."*

6. Personal Appeals

Personal appeals focus on other people. They assume a form of relationship and a degree of trust between a leader and followers. Using personal appeals asks others to do something out of friendship or asks for a favor before clarifying it. They might say:

- *"We both go back a long time with this company. I would like your help on ..."*
- *"I need to ask for a favor ..."*
- *"Can I count on you making ... ?"*

7. Exchanging

Exchanging focuses more on other people because it assumes that the leader knows what is valuable and important to those he influences. A leader using this influence tactic gives something of value to the people he is leading in return for something they want. A leader who is exchanging might say things like:

- *"If you support the decision, I will support your request ..."*

- *"In return for your participation in this survey, I will send you the aggregated results."*

8. Consultation

Consultation also focuses on other people. The leader pulls their target in and engages them to come up with a course of action. They ask the target to suggest improvements or help plan an activity. Typical statements by a leader using consultation influence tactics include:

- *"I suggest that we do XYZ. What do you suggest?"*
- *"Knowing the industry, do you think the merger is the best choice?"*
- *"In your opinion, what would be the pros and cons?"*

9. Inspirational Appeals

Inspiring is almost the exact opposite of rational persuasion. The leader focuses on the heart rather than the head. They appeal to emotions and suggest the possibilities if only the target were persuaded. Inspirational appeals are by far the most personal influence tactic. The leader has to understand other people's perspectives to focus on their internal motivators, values and emotions. They might use statements like:

- *"Since you care for the development of children, I would like to take you aboard the elementary education project."*
- *"You are the best one to handle the negotiation because you care about being both businesslike and environmentally sensitive."*

ASSESSING THE EFFECTIVENESS OF YOUR APPROACH

Research has found "rational" to be the most commonly applied influence tactic. In one experiment, people were lined up at a copy machine. Another person joined the line and requested to go to the head of the line. 63% of the people in the queue agreed. The line jumper was required to make a change to his request. Instead, he asked, "May I go to the head of the line because I have copies to make?". 90% of the people agreed to let him jump. Only the "because" phrase was different in the second request. Other studies have proven that rationality is related to positive outcomes in the workplace.

Even though most leaders use rational persuasion, the tactic has a low commitment rate of 23%. Leaders using inspirational appeals get a 90% commitment rate followed by consultation with a commitment rate of 55%. No effective leader uses just one persuasion tactic, though. Too much dependence on any one tactic will cause it to lose its effectiveness. You judge the effectiveness of an influence tactic by distinguishing among three possible outcomes – compliance, commitment or resistance in the target.

Once a leader has picked an influence tactic, the follower's response determines its success. The follower can resist the leader's efforts to influence him, and this happens in different forms such as:

- Refusing to oblige
- Making excuses for why they cannot oblige
- Delaying the action required of them
- Asking higher authorities to overrule the decision
- Faking compliance and then trying to sabotage the decision
- Trying to change the leader's mind about the action

The leader could also get an unenthusiastic compliance from the follower. In such a case, their behavior has been influenced, but their attitude remains unchanged. The third possible outcome is a commitment from the target. The committed follower has accepted influence and is voluntarily making an effort to perform the required action.

Consider the following situational examples of effective influence tactics:

Situation A

You are the CEO of your company and concerned that some managers within your organization do not understand why they need to be competitive. The profit and loss statement shows that the performance of the business has been steadily slipping. Still, most of your managers do not think there is a need for change. You are wondering what approach to use to push a total quality program. In this scenario, the goal is to influence employees to see the connection between motivation and economic gain. Your best bet could be using personal and inspirational appeals to influence a long-term behavior change. You will lower your chances of success significantly if you use hard tactics like requesting, legitimating and coalition.

Situation B

You chair the Administrative Council in your local community. After analyzing the financial report at the end of the year, you find that the budget needs to be increased by $10,000 to match insurance premiums. You must talk to the members to influence them to give more. You would be best served by using inspirational appeals and rational persuasion. Again, hard tactics would be the least effective method to use.

Research has found that soft tactics typically yield the most commitment. Followers or targets of the persuasion become convinced and take up action of their own volition. Combining soft tactics with rational appeals was the second-most effective approach, while hard tactics were the least effective. A leader will often have to choose between influence tactics to help meet organizational goals. They must be able to determine the best tactic for each situation, group or person.

A transformational wizard and warrior leader will recognize that they must motivate their team. They will want to create a "commitment culture" that begins by modeling personal values and using tactics that allow followers to choose to follow them enthusiastically. When leaders behave in a truly inspirational manner, employees will be more committed, productive and satisfied than those following leaders who do not "walk the talk." A study involving 100,000 assessments on 8,000 leaders found that "inspiring and motivating others to high performance" is the leadership quality that most accurately differentiates high and low performers. It proves that hard tactics often produce zero commitment.

A transformational leader establishes the direction and the organizational objectives. They make those objectives larger than life to offer real purpose and meaning to the team's work. As a result, they get team members who can see the value of their individual and collective contributions to the organization's vision and mission.

5

ADVERSITY

Often, great leaders are celebrated for their success. Paradoxically, they become great because of the trials of failure. The lessons they learned while confronting uncertainty and fear and from frustration made them great. A transformational leader knows how to turn adversity into opportunity and does this effectively for the sake of growth and development. Their best behavior is authenticity. They do not pretend to be someone else. They know that lack of authenticity is draining and can leave you isolated and lonely.

In today's social media world, everyone is highly networked. You are constantly bombarded with images of people who are doing exceptionally well, at least according to their profiles, which do not sometimes match real life. The pressure for perfection is real. No wonder many people find it easy to operate under pretenses. Being transparent and authentic does not make you a lesser leader. It can make you a more decisive leader who knows how to persevere and overcome challenges. It proves to you and your followers that you do not quit when faced with adversity; you can accomplish great things despite being in a difficult situation. It also displays a willingness to get help from others when you need it.

A considerable part of authenticity is admitting to your imperfections and showing your vulnerability. In leadership, vulnerability is not a new idea. Since it was first discussed in academic circles in 2010, the concept has continually been developed. Some experts talk a great deal about the need for vulnerability, yet the idea has not been accepted as much as it ought to be. A leader who does not understand vulnerability cannot lead and manage people. People are not even open to following you if you are not vulnerable.

When you show authentic vulnerability, your employees get to see the real you. Research shows that transparency from senior leaders helps to build employee trust. Trust is the most challenging element to cultivate in the workplace and the most powerful contributor to workplace wellbeing. Other than a 'sense of purpose,' trust contributes the most to workplace happiness. The findings on transparency do not just touch on the senior leaders alone, though. Employees who trust a person in authority are likely to bring creativity, positive energy, and motivation to their work which translates in low turnover.

Of course, showing up authentically vulnerable has its risks. A lot is riding on it. For example, if you tell your employees that you do not have answers but are working to find them, in some cases, like in a pandemic, that would provide them comfort. Vulnerability becomes strength. Imagine, though, if you told your employees that you have no idea how to work during the same crisis, how do you think they would respond? Admitting that you do not have resources during a crisis can only breed chaos and damage your credibility.

In leadership, vulnerability starts with sincerity and selflessness in your intentions. That way, any display of vulnerability comes from a place of compassion towards others and yourself. Leading vulnerably is not about driving business value or getting better sales. It is about embodying humanity in your leadership. You are not a perfect person; you have your struggles like other people. Leading with vulnerability is showing people that you sincerely understand their challenges and empathize. Ultimately, vulnerability will connect you with your team.

In its very nature, vulnerability demands risk. It requires that you step out and show yourself in a way that exposes you. There is no guarantee that you will be successful. As such, you will require courage. You will need to learn to step out of your comfort zone regularly and when the situation calls for it. A transformational leader can create a culture where discomfort in this sense helps you move forward and become more productive. They normalize vulnerability in their office and encourage learning. It is worth noting here that you do not have to share all the facets of your life with the people you lead in being vulnerable. You do not have to share your deepest fears.

One way to manage the risks of leading with vulnerability is to have boundaries around what is helpful in the workplace and what is not. Vulnerability without limitations is simply undisciplined oversharing. While as a leader, you need a place where you can be truly who you are and share your thoughts without censure, that place is not the office. Ideally, the vulnerable leader can use their vulnerability to create a space where the workforce can do the same.

COPING WITH TOUGH TIMES

Progress is always tied to challenges. Few businesses can keep growing and expanding without occasional challenges. The road bump could be short-lived, or it may take some time to deal with. Still, all setbacks test your leadership mettle. Employees are always looking at you to be reassured that things will turn out just fine. As such, you have to figure out how to deal with negative people, how to handle rumors, and how to stay composed and confident even when you are uncertain. The thing that sets successful people apart from everyone else is their ability to remain confident and sustain power during uncertain periods. To do this:

Maintain Rational Optimism

When people feel rationally positive, they perform better. A positive mental state produces higher productivity and creativity, which means that if you are not sure how a project is going or its outcome, keeping an optimistic mindset could foster the creative insight you need to be successful. It also boosts your confidence when you are uncertain.

Atomize Your Plans

Whenever you are working towards something in life, map out different potential outcomes. Having only one possible path to reach the goal could make you anxious. After all, what will you do if you fail? If you map out different routes, you will feel confident that the outcome is possible anyway.

View Uncertainty Like a Chance to Grow

Sometimes, things look bad at the moment, and then, in retrospect, you are happy that things went as they did. This is a reality of life – embrace it. The universe supports you and wants you to do well. Even when you do not know the best way to reach your goal, you can afford to calmly try and work it out, knowing that in the end, it will all be good. Learn to think of those moments of uncertainty as opportunities to grow, and you will start to believe that they are working in your favor.

Do the Best You Can

One of the most helpful ways to keep confidence in uncertainty is knowing that you have done the best that you could. That way, you can let go of what is outside of your control. Many people make the mistake of giving their all in love or work and then stressing as they wait to see whether the result will be as they hoped. You can escape this trap by always doing your best and leaving the rest to play out as it would.

You must build self-confidence in all this because if you do not believe in yourself, who will? How will you guide others towards the future you hope for if you don't believe that you can? Self-confidence fuels your determination. It helps you to stay the course even when you are facing setbacks. It is the knowledge that you can do whatever you set your mind to, and the surety that you can lead your team to a successful future. Displaying self-confidence in the workplace boosts employee morale. It makes you fearless, knowing that you can do whatever you need to do without second-guessing yourself.

The self-confident leader communicates with confidence. Regardless of who their audience may be, they are always confident of their abilities. As a self-confident leader, you know that you can keep your integrity at all times. You are aware of what is appropriate in conversation, and you can deal with whatever comes your way. As such, you become a conduit for ideas. You believe in your employees; you can listen to their opinions, reward those who do well and believe that every output has value.

Self-confidence will increase your self-assurance. You will not have to deal with insecurity since you know your capabilities. You know that you are fitting for the job, and so when others doubt your abilities, it does not faze you. Instead, you prove them wrong and win them over, which boosts your abilities and skills and enhances your satisfaction with your work. Self-confidence is the gift that keeps on giving. It fuels you to aim higher and to become better. It keeps you calm and composed even when you have to take risks. It allows you to respond well to criticism and to use it as fuel and feedback to become better. How then do you build self-confidence?

a. Find Your Passion

To make a difference, you have to go beyond other people's expectations, which demands that you be motivated from within. Finding your passion will provide this incentive. What is it that wakes you up in the morning ready to conquer the world? What can you not have enough of? Intrinsic motivation will drive you to be different.

b. Act Independently

Some people make it their job to complain, waiting for others to take action. No great leader is a complainer. Work on your ideas. Do what you need to make them a reality. Leaders execute. So, if a problem presents itself to you, work on fixing it.

c. Rethink Risk

It is easy to imagine that because most people fail to act, there is risk involved in an action. However, inaction is often the riskiest option. To make a difference, you have to focus on helping others and making them better. In doing so, they see the leadership qualities in you and are more confident to follow you.

Seek Respect over Being Liked

If you make decisions in your life based on what other people think of you, your life will not be your own. If you cannot live your life, you cannot impact others. Quit worrying about being liked and focus on respect. Leaders have many choices to make, and all of them will not be received well. Cultivate the discipline to make decisions because they are right.

Know the Legacy You Hope for

Do not wait until the situation is ideal to begin working towards a goal you want. The time to make a difference is now. If you wait for permission from others, you will have long to wait. Begin writing the story you want others to remember you by now.

DEALING WITH MISTAKES

As you work on your leadership skills and influence other people to be more innovative, mistakes are bound to happen in the workplace. Either you or your people will blunder at one point, and it helps to know how to deal with these mistakes. How you handle them shows who you are as a leader. If you are the one who makes a mistake, learn from it. Some of the most significant lessons in life come from missteps. Reflect on what you could have done to avoid the mistake. That way, you know how to avoid the same traps in the future. As you do so, make sure to own the mistake. Your employees are watching to see how you handle it. If you cannot admit to yourself and others when you are wrong, you do more damage.

Avoid beating yourself up for the mistake, though. You are just as human as everyone else. Instead, if you find yourself leaning towards berating yourself, take a break. Remove yourself from the situation and return when you are calm; it will give you a fresh perspective. Alternatively, talk to another person about it. Make sure it is someone who can call you out when you are to blame. They will help you clarify issues.

Learning from your mistake is not complete until you begin to make amends for the mistake. This may mean anything from removing processes you had introduced at work to issuing an apology to the people most affected by the mistake. Ensure that you find out how you can avoid the mistake in the future and how you can minimize damage caused by the mistake. When you have done these things, let it go. Commit to the lesson learned and do not ruminate on the mistake more than you need to. It could make you afraid, and fear could trigger more mistakes.

The whole idea of transformational leadership is to change mistakes into opportunities. It is to model behavior for those around you to teach them how to handle their mistakes and those of others better. Demonstrate leadership when you make a mistake by:

Acknowledging the Mistake

Never blame others or try to cover up what you did wrong. Own your mess and admit it. It is the insecure leader who will be afraid of looking weak by admitting their mistake. Admitting your mistake is one way to be vulnerable, and vulnerability, as discussed earlier, is a strength. It will earn you respect from others and humanize you.

Teach Others the Lessons You Learned from Your Mistake

Learning from the mistake means that you do whatever is necessary so that you do not repeat it. It also means that you inspire those that you are leading not to repeat the same mistakes. Teach your employees what you have learned in a way that builds trust and connection. Remember that the best leaders are guides and coaches; they show others the way after they have walked it.

The way that you make mistakes is the same way that others will make mistakes. How do you deal with the mistakes of others? What can you learn from your mistakes to help you deal better with other people's mistakes? Your response to other people's mistakes can vary from showing empathy to firing. Here are eight tips to help you handle other people's mistakes:

Deal with the Mistake Quickly

Leaving a mistake unaddressed could have numerous consequences. What might have been easily resolvable could spiral and affect other departments and people, causing unexpected revenue and trust losses. Address the mistake as fast as you can.

Deal with the Issue Clinically

Make sure you handle the situation with care. For example, shouting at the employee from your office after learning about the mistake might not help them do better or earn you respect. Call the involved parties aside. Do not use intimidation tactics in a bid to rush a solution.

Collect All the Facts

Find out how the mistake happened. Who was involved? What was their thought process? Did the mistake happen because of communication issues or process issues? What other factors contributed to the mistake? Find out all the details you can regarding the mistake.

Confront the Issue, Not the Person

Do not make your resolution personal. Do not attack their character or personality. Instead, deal with the issue as separate from their person as you can.

Treat Them with Compassion

In some cases, the mistake could be due to personality or character issues. In such cases, compassion will be your best bet. Always remember that you make mistakes as well, and it will help you to be kind in unpacking the mistake.

Turn the Negative into Positive

The mistake is damaging; otherwise, it would not be a mistake. Turn it around by finding out ways to learn from it. Help your employee to figure out what they could have done better. If applicable, put in place processes to avoid repeating the mistake in the future. To do this, you will need to establish whether the mistake was primarily caused by a lack of training or an attitude issue. Address the root cause appropriately.

Follow up

Following up on the mistake does not mean reminding your employee what they did wrong. It means checking up on the processes you put in place to ensure that the mistake does not happen again. Are they working? Do they need to be adjusted?

CONFLICT MANAGEMENT AND PROBLEM SOLVING

Conflict can occur within groups or between people in different situations. People are different in personality, culture, character, and beliefs, so conflict is only natural if there is effective interaction. It is neither a good thing nor a bad thing. It is simply a necessary part of building meaningful relationships within groups and with people. Conflict can be divided into three types:

- Economic Conflict – Here, there are competing motives in the attainment of strained resources. Each party is often concerned with increasing their gain.
- Value Conflict – Parties involved in a value conflict are incompatible in the way they live. They have different ideologies and principles.
- Power Conflict – In a power conflict, each party tries to exert and keep its maximum influence in the social setting or relationship. If one party has more influence, they may win the power struggle and lose the relationship. Parties are often trying to control each other.

In the workplace, conflict can result from gender, race, attitude, opinions, religion, feelings, and cultures. It could also come up from differences in positions, affiliations, status, roles, and values. Often in one conflict, the sources are different. As a leader, thinking of conflict as an opportunity to learn and grow may lead to positive outcomes. It will help you think of effective conflict resolution and management. Since the emotions resulting from conflict are often uncomfortable, many people avoid it, but dealing with conflict gives you a better understanding of others, better working relationships, better solutions, and higher team performances due to increased motivation. There are generally four levels of conflict, including:

1. Interpersonal Conflict – This happens when two people in a relationship have differing approaches or goals. Compromise is necessary to manage this type of conflict and foster growth.
2. Intrapersonal Conflict – Intrapersonal conflict is internal. It happens when a person has different emotions, principles, values, and desires. If they have difficulties interpreting their feelings, it can be challenging to resolve this conflict. It could spiral to anxiety and depression and can create other conflict levels.
3. Intergroup Conflict – There is an intergroup conflict if two separate teams in an organization cannot agree. This could be because they are competing for resources, have different interests, or even because their group identity is threatened. This conflict can escalate fast and can cause huge losses for an organization. If managed well, it can result in remarkable progress for the organization.
4. Intragroup Conflict – This is conflict between individuals within the same team. If managed well, it can cause the team to grow towards

achieving its goals. Otherwise, it can disrupt the entire team and slow productivity.

No matter the conflict level, there are methods you can employ to manage conflict. Conflict management is the process of reducing the unwanted outcomes of conflict and increasing positive results. There are different models that leaders can use, but this section covers the most popular style: the Thomas-Kilmann Conflict Mode Instrument, referred to as TKI from here on.

TKI is an assessment tool that you can use to measure a person's behavior during conflict. It provides feedback on how effectively a person can use different conflict-handling modes. It is based on assertiveness and cooperativeness so that all the modes fall within a scale from being assertive to being cooperative. They include:

1. Avoiding

A leader who avoids is low on assertiveness and cooperativeness. They withdraw from conflict, and so no one wins. They neither assert their concerns nor seek to address other people's. Such leaders may adopt a passive attitude hoping that the conflict will just go away, but conflict-avoidance can cause larger issues. This mode is only useful when emotions are high, and people need to calm down or when the problem is not worth disagreeing over. You can also apply this mode if the team can resolve the conflict without your involvement or when avoiding the conflict has more benefits than addressing it.

2. Accommodating

Accommodating is high in cooperation and low in assertiveness. You ignore your concerns for the sake of other people's needs. You sacrifice what you need for the sake of peace, and so you lose, and the other person wins. This mode can provide an immediate solution but could make you seem like a pushover. Use this mode when a person realizes their mistake and accepts another solution, when the issue is more significant to them, so that it is a show of goodwill on your side and when pushing your agenda could cause damage. Accommodating can also come in handy when you want to let the team learn from its mistakes. Do not accommodate if the result is vital to the team's success.

3. Competing

Competing is high in assertiveness and low on cooperation. You meet your needs at the expense of your team. You use any power you have to win. This mode can be necessary in some cases, but misusing it can cause more conflict. Use this mode when you need an immediate decision, when you cannot compromise an outcome or when you need to demonstrate strong leadership and take unpopular action. You can also apply it when the welfare of the business is at stake. Avoid it when you could face retaliation or weakened support.

4. Collaborating

Collaborating is highly cooperative and assertive. Both the parties in conflict win. You work with the team to find a solution that addresses both concerns. Collaborating requires a lot of resources, energy, and time. It can cause positive outcomes, better creativity, and a stronger team structure. Collaborate when the two parties are too important for compromise, when the conflict affects team dynamics, or when you want to improve commitment. Collaborating can also be useful to merge ideas and viewpoints. Avoid it when working with limited resources, energy, and time or when you need a quick decision.

5. Compromising

Compromising is moderate on cooperativeness and assertiveness. Each party gives up more than they would prefer so that only part of their concerns are met. No one loses or wins, but an acceptable solution is reached. Using this mode can create a middle ground but could cause others to take advantage of you. It can also cause an outcome that is less than optimal. Compromising is effective when you need a quick decision on a complex matter, when the conflicting parties are equal in rank or power, and when other modes fail. Avoid this mode when partial satisfaction could cause your team to take advantage of you.

A leader's role in conflict management can affect organizational conflict management culture. Research shows that leaders spend over 20% of their time dealing with conflict. A common trait among great leaders is building a team that works well together and facilitates conflict resolution. They are leaders in conflict management. To be an effective leader, you have to assess the necessary action and intervene to meet the demand. Transformational leaders lead conflict management and resolution by:

- Honesty – They do not hesitate to speak about things that need discussing.

- Receptivity – They seek to understand team members, knowing that conflict is okay and listening to the opinions of others is not a sign of weakness.
- Depersonalization – They remove personal feeling from team conflict.
- Listening – They listen carefully and offer feedback.
- Clarity – Transformational leaders ensure that everyone understands how decisions are made during conflict resolution.
- Outlaw Triangulation – They do not allow team members to gang up on others.
- Accountability – They follow through on their words and hold others accountable.
- Reward and Recognition – Transformational leaders recognize successful conflict management and offer a reward for it.

6

INSPIRATION

By definition, a transformational leader inspires their people. The word 'inspire' translates to 'in spirit.' Inspiration comes from within. It pulls you toward something that stirs your mind and heart. When inspired, we are not thinking about the result; we do not need external validation to proceed. The feeling of meaning and purpose propels us forward. The transformational leader provides this. They know how to infuse commitment, passion, energy, and connection to the organization, primarily through empathy.

To be empathetic, though, you must understand how to read others and understand what motivates them. The inspiring leader seeks to understand other people's motivations to get them to commit to action. They do this by working on the driving factors for people's inner motivators, empowering them to act.

UNDERSTANDING WHAT MOTIVATES PEOPLE

People often assume that what motivates a leader is the same thing that motivates their people, but this assumption can affect team dynamics. Highly motivated people are more likely to perform better and to be more productive. They are less likely to leave, and so understanding other people's motivations will help your organization. To understand the people you work with, know who they are, and empathize.

Each of us has different events and circumstances that shaped us to become who we are. Those events are coded into our inner world. They inform our routines and beliefs, which further influence the way we experience life and how we behave. Everyone's inner world is made of different assumptions along with emotional and mental patterns that are unique. Each person has five layers:

1. Personality

Personality theories are the mainstream approach to understanding mindsets. These theories focus on explaining behaviors that individuals exhibit consistently over time. They predict human reactions to other people, as well as stress, crises, and problems. Many psychologists believe that there are five personality dimensions, including:

Extraversion

An extraverted person is friendly, excitable, assertive, talkative, and highly expressive. They are outgoing, drawing their energy from social situations. People high in extraversion feel energized being around others; they love being the center of attention, meeting new people, and starting conversations. They often say things without first considering them. If you are low in extraversion, you are reserved and find social events draining. Introverted people require quiet and solitude to rest; they dislike small talk, being in the limelight, and always consider what they say before speaking.

Agreeableness

Agreeableness includes traits like affection, altruism, kindness, and trust. Highly agreeable people are more cooperative. They help those who need it, care for others, enjoy making other people happy and feel empathy for others. Less agreeable people are competitive and often manipulative. They have little interest in other people, often belittling and insulting them. They do not care about the feelings of others.

Openness

Openness includes characteristics like insight and imagination. People high in openness have many interests because they are curious. They are creative, focused, open to learning, and happy to entertain abstract ideas. People who are low in openness are traditional. They resist new ideas, dislike change, and do not enjoy talking about theoretical concepts.

Conscientiousness

Conscientiousness is about impulse control, thoughtfulness, and goal orientation. The highly conscientious are organized, detail-oriented, and enjoy planning. They finish the essential tasks first. Less conscientious people do not like schedules. They postpone important tasks and often fail to finish their assigned tasks.

Neuroticism

Neuroticism is characterized by moodiness, emotional instability, and sadness. Highly neurotic people experience mood swings, sadness, irritability, and anxiety. They are easily upset, and they struggle to recover after stressful events, constantly worrying about various things. People low in neuroticism are more emotionally resilient and stable. They know how to handle stress and how to stay relaxed. They do not worry about much.

The Big Five Traits are universal. Research on how they are distributed across 50 cultures found the dimensions to describe personality accurately. Knowing where your team members fall on the personality scale can help you to inspire them better.

2. Context

When trying to understand what motivates a person, it pays to consider their situation or context. To do this, answer the following questions:

- What are their possible motivations? What is at stake?
- What do other people expect from them?
- What is the context and structure in the organization, and who is their boss? Who do they influence? Which team do they belong to, and who are the other members?
- What is the organizational culture? (Culture has a lot of significance. For example, a person working in an organization where people follow through on their commitments is more likely to be conscientious.)
- What are the interpersonal and group dynamics? (People do not act in isolation often; they generally act in relationships with others.)
- How do other people perceive this person?
- Are they under pressure?

3. Know-how

People are more likely to behave in line with what they know and with their past positive experiences. Know-how and experiences that are relevant to leaders in a corporate context may include:

- Understanding the industry's value drivers and trends.
- Understanding the customers and the growth markets. (For example, a supply chain manager knows emerging markets).
- Having the relevant technical knowledge (such as expertise in marketing or R&D).
- Having the relevant education (some jobs require a scientific background).

To diagnose a person's behavioral tendencies, you can ask questions like:

- What did the person do in the past?
- What units and functions did they run?
- Was the person successful in running those units?
- Has the person been in a similar situation to the one facing them today? (For instance, was the person already a leader in a turnaround situation?) What did the person do? Was it successful? How did they behave then?

4. Skills

People typically behave in ways that build on their skills and abilities. Ask yourself what skills and abilities a person has. Common skills you can watch out for include:

- Solving complex problems effectively
- Making sound decisions
- Building high-performance teams
- Communicating positively and engaging the organization
- Inspiring others towards higher performance

5. Values, Emotions, and Emotional Dispositions

Values and priorities reflect a person's sense of right and wrong, good and evil, what is important and unimportant, or what "ought" to be. Some values are physiologically determined, and people typically consider them objective, such as the desire to avoid physical pain or seek pleasure. Other values are seen as subjective, and they vary across individuals and cultures: moral, ideological, religious, political, and social.

If you want to lead others, you must understand their values. Otherwise, you will have difficulties presenting your vision in a way that means something to them. You must understand their value systems and their emotions. You can ask others how they feel to understand their emotions, but it does not have to end there. Observing their non-verbal communication and behavior will provide more understanding. According to Paul Eckman, six basic universal emotions influence how we interact with others. They include:

1. Happiness

Of all emotions, people strive the most for happiness. By definition, happiness is a pleasant emotional state connected with joy, well-being, satisfaction, contentment, and gratification. A happy person may smile, have relaxed body language and speak positively. While happiness is basic, the things that create it are influenced by culture. Pop culture, for example, suggests that the more you have, the happier you are. Other cultures link status and happiness. Either way, research suggests that happiness plays a role in mental and physical health. It is linked to increased marital satisfaction and longevity.

2. Sadness

Sadness is characterized by feelings of grief, hopelessness, disappointment, and disinterest. It is a transient emotion, but sometimes people experience it for prolonged periods, turning into depression. A sad person might withdraw from others, cry, keep quiet and experience lethargy. How sad you feel depends on the reason.

3. Fear

Fear can play a significant role in survival. When you are afraid, you either flee or fight, both of which are fear responses. Your heart rate increases, muscles become tense, and your mind becomes alert. Fear is typically expressed through physiological reactions like rapid breathing, widening eyes, and attempts to flee or hide from the threat. Like other emotions, no one experiences fear the same way. Particular objects or situations trigger some people, but the underlying fact is a real or perceived threat. Others are thrill-seekers who seek out situations that provoke fear, like in extreme sports.

4. Disgust

People turn away in disgust. You can see it through physical reactions like retching or facial expressions such as curling the upper lip. Disgust typically comes from an unpleasant smell, sight, or taste, but people experience disgust when they see others doing something they consider evil, immoral or distasteful.

5. Anger

Anger is characterized by feeling agitated, hostile, antagonistic, or frustrated. It is displayed through facial expressions like glaring, body language like looking aside, aggressive behaviors, physiological responses like sweating, and tone of voice. People often think of anger as negative, but it can be a good thing when it helps to clarify one's needs and fuels problem-solving. If expressed in unhealthy and aggressive ways, it becomes a problem.

6. Surprise

Surprise is characterized by a startled response to the unexpected. It can be neutral, negative, or positive. A surprised person could gasp or scream, they might jump back, and their facial expressions will include widened eyes and raised eyebrows.

The six basic emotions combine to form different feelings like amusement, contempt, guilt, relief, and shame. In that sense, no emotion exists as an island. Many emotions you experience are complex and nuanced. They work together to create a broad palette of human emotional life. The easiest categorization of emotions is negative or positive emotions. The point is not that some emotions are good and others bad, but that some emotions can quickly spiral out of control. The categories are more to do with the actions attached to the emotions than the emotions themselves.

Many people believe that negative emotions cause ineffective and dysfunctional behavior, but in the ordinary and non-extreme intensities, negative emotions are necessary for normal human functioning. For example, without a negative emotion like fear, compassion might not make sense. Fear is vital in fleeing from danger or fighting to protect oneself.

Other than their values and emotions, people's behavior is also motivated by their emotional disposition. Emotional disposition is the tendency to have a particular type of affective experience, most often toward the type of experience the person has already had. It is a continual leaning towards certain emotions around a specific object. For example, if a child continually pulls the cat's tail, the cat can develop a permanent tendency to be angry whenever the child is nearby. The same way emotions influence behavior, emotional dispositions influence patterns of behavior. Observing these patterns may give us clues about another person's emotional disposition, even before we meet. A person's emotional disposition may be linked to their personality type.

The five aspects or layers to a person influence how they behave and how they react in different situations. As a leader, knowing each individual in your team will help you to tailor your approaches. You can determine the best ways to achieve satisfaction, motivation, and commitment.

INSPIRE THROUGH EMPATHY

In a debate in 1992, President Bill Clinton said, "I feel your pain," a statement that garnered a lot of attention. It suggested empathy and humanized him, making him appear to be in touch with his people. Media outlets wondered whether he meant his words. The honesty of politicians (or lack of) aside, would it be a good thing or a bad thing to feel someone else's pain?

In leadership, empathy allows you to understand what motivates other people better. It is the glue that fosters connection with these people, making you appear personable. Empathy allows you to acknowledge others for who they are and, from there, positively influence them to make necessary changes to their behavior. It earns their commitment. It gives you the effective and cognitive skill to recognize, appreciate, and interpret others' feelings. Empathy requires the ability to experience the world subjectively from another person's perspective. It doesn't mean understanding how it would feel to walk in the other person's shoes. Instead, it is the ability to sense and connect to the other person's inner motivators and the factors driving those motivators. Psychologists have suggested three types of empathy:

- Perspective-taking – This type of empathy is

purely cognitive. You use your mind to try and see things from another person's perspective. You put on, as it were, their shoes and walk a mile in them.

- Personal Distress – The type of empathy Bill Clinton displayed in his comment is personal distress. It is literally feeling another person's emotions. It is the kind of empathy you feel when you resonate with a character in a movie.

- Empathic Concern – Empathic concern is the ability to recognize the emotional state someone else is in, feel in tune with it and show the appropriate concern. It is the type of empathy you want to cultivate as a leader.

There are different ways to develop empathic concern personally, and they are influenced by genetics, temperament, parenting, and neuro-developmental factors. These strategies can help you to empathize with others and, in effect, lead better.

1. Nurture Curiosity

Embrace a curiosity towards the people you influence. Schedule time to spend with those you do not know well and ask them personal questions about their life, welfare, and personalities. On social media, interact with people from different backgrounds and consider what they have to say. If you can, visit new places and meet new people as you immerse yourself in their cultures.

2. Leave Your Comfort Zone

Pick up a book and learn a new thing that is outside of your comfort zone. The idea is to find out what you are like when confronted with something you do not know. Find support if you need it and accept the helplessness that comes with your limitations. It will humble you, and humility is a path to being empathic.

3. Solicit and Accept Feedback

Ask your family, friends, and colleagues to give you feedback about your relationship and listening skills. Where could you improve? What opportunities do you fail to see?

4. Confront Your Biases

Everyone has biases that impact their capacity to be empathic. We often judge other people without realizing it. Find ways to interact with people who are different from you and discuss important issues. Find what you have in common and express interest without judgment. Understand what it feels like to be in their life, work and experiences. Nurture relationships with people you would otherwise not interact with.

5. Have Difficult but Respectful Conversations

It is difficult to challenge others or deal with challenges to your perspective, but willingly entering those conversations can help you build empathy. Listen without interrupting, keep an open mind and apologize when you hurt another person's feelings with your words. If an issue is new to you, research and understand the origins of a perspective and its impact on others.

6. Join a Cause

Researchers have found that collaborating on community projects can remove biases and heal divisions and differences. Find a community you like and a cause you believe in and join it. Participate alongside others and be open to learning.

7. Read as Much as You Can

Read and read widely. Read journals, newspapers, non-fiction, fiction, and online content from different backgrounds and across different subjects. This will increase your capacity for empathy and your emotional intelligence. Seek out writers whose stories are unique and enter the inner worlds of their characters.

HOW TO APPLY EMPATHY IN THE WORKPLACE

Listen Well

Empathetic leaders do not just listen; they listen well. True listening means listening with an open heart. It is paying attention to a person's tone, body language, and other hidden emotions behind their words. When you listen well, you are not trying to develop a rebuttal – you genuinely try to see the other person's perspective.

Do Not Interrupt

Empathetic leaders understand that distractions can lower the quality of a conversation. The distracted listener grows frustrated and impatient. They interrupt the speaker as they try to move them along their message. Try not to cut people off. Give them space to say what they need to say.

Be Present

The empathetic leader does not glance at their watch every few seconds or check their phone for updates in the middle of a conversation. When someone is talking to you, listen. Be fully there. Concentrate on their words and show support.

Listen without Judgment

Even when other people's opinions and feelings differ from yours, do not judge. Leave your biases aside. It will help you to see new perspectives. It will allow you to see the feelings of others as an opportunity to understand them better and connect.

Encourage Those Who Are Quiet

In meetings, there will always be some people who do not talk much. The empathic leader knows how to encourage them to voice their opinions. That way, you empower them to be heard.

7

COMMITMENT

I n an earlier chapter, we mentioned that the inspiring transformational leader:

- Understands what motivates people
- Gets them to commit to action by connecting to their inner motivators
- Empowers them to act

In this chapter, we will discuss how to maximize commitment. How do you get people to commit to action?

Leading people along a broad group dynamic is one of the challenges many leaders face. The transformational leader builds strong non-verbal and verbal relationships within their team to build trust. They know how to build effective teams, creating solid professional relationships characterized by straightforward communication.

THE ROLE MODELING WIZARD

As a leader in your business, you should present the right message to your colleagues, customers, employees, and business partners. Your staff expects you to lead by example. Through role modeling, you can exemplify and transform other people's values. You may assume that your work speaks for itself, but how you present yourself and the things to which you give your time also matter. The same way you make judgments about other people you meet is the same way others do about you. To transform others, you have to take advantage of identification – the process where the influenced person assimilates an attribute or value from the leader. For it to work, you have to be a person whose social role others aspire to play. The following are five ways you can begin leading by example:

Get to Work Early

If you arrive at your work late regularly, employees begin to assume that they can do the same. They assume a lower value for the work you do. In leadership, exemplify the traits you would want in your employees. The work ethic in your workplace can be influenced by what you do, and so if they see you arrive early every day, they are likely to mirror that trait.

Express the Organizational Brand

Make sure you personify your company's brand even in your online presence. Set aside some time to update your social media profiles and website to make sure they reflect your business beliefs accurately and positively. Ensure that your employees maintain the promise your brand makes to the world.

Look the Part

What you choose to wear is your way of presenting yourself to the world; it can communicate to others your competence, knowledge, and other aspects about yourself. Make good wardrobe choices – invest in clothes that fit the part and match your business and its industry.

Share Credit

You cannot succeed in business by working alone forever. Collaboration is necessary. You lose the respect of your colleagues and employees if you cannot share the spotlight. When other people do well, recognize their accomplishments and praise them generously. It causes higher motivation and inspires them to do better.

Perfect Your Listening Skills

Transformational leaders need the skill of listening. Work to better your listening skills. Make eye contact, listen attentively and ask relevant questions. Insist that your employees do the same. It will create a culture of respect and consideration in the workplace.

EMOTIONS ARE CONTAGIOUS

Emotional contagion happens when a person's emotions and related behaviors influence similar behaviors and emotions in others. A leader can influence other people's emotions by consciously spreading the emotions they like by building empathy, among other things. G. Schoenewolf described emotional contagion as behavioral induction in people and groups. It happens through subconscious mimicry and synchronization of a person's expressions, postures, movements, and vocalizations.

As such, it can be positive or negative. During strikes, people are often stirred to violence and anger by an influencer, which is an example of emotional contagion. A positive example is when a leader constantly smiles, inspiring positive feelings in the workforce. Research has found that mimicry is natural during social interaction. In the 1990s, scientists discovered that the brain of a monkey watching another pick up something and the monkey that picked the object up fired the same neurons. These processes also occur between people.

Mirror neurons strengthen the more activated they get. Emotional contagion often connects and fuses people with others in a way that you can 'lose yourself' to other people's emotions. The concept of emotional contagion has implications for the leader. The leader can find ways to spread positivity in the workplace. They can express gratitude and encourage others to mirror it. Emotional contagion means that the leader's attitudes go into work every day and seep through the whole work environment. It also means that there are ways you can practice it with intentionality. You can take advantage of body language communication.

People imitate people. If someone smiles at you, you smile back. In an earlier chapter, we discussed non-verbal communication. Being aware of the message you are sending in your non-verbal communication can go a long way in helping you to take advantage of emotional contagion. Since higher energy pulls more attention, the same emotion expressed with high energy becomes more contagious. This is to say that the leader using emotional contagion can galvanize others using positive energy and emotions. They show commitment, enthusiasm, passion, and dedication.

Their stories are exciting and inspiring, painting an energizing vision of the future.

In short, if you harness the power of your emotions, you harness the power of your team. You can choose how you want to feel and the emotion you would like to pass to others. Suppose you want to feel peaceful, hopeful, happy, and loving and invite others to feel the same way; you can decide to use your facial expressions and body language to communicate those emotions. That way, you infect people positively. In the words of Oprah Winfrey, "You can take responsibility for the energy you bring into a space."

Reward and Recognition

The rewards given by senior executives have a major impact on the performance culture in an organization. They send a clear message about the specific behaviors that are valued and can maximize commitment. The benefits of reward and recognition are motivational and significant, and they often cost very little. To enhance the effectiveness of rewards and recognition:

Focus on Strategy

The time you spend planning and crystalizing outcomes is critical. Thoughtfully identify the areas that need improvement, whether staff retention, sales, or customer service metrics. It will help you design an effective program and to identify what you are doing right and who needs to be recognized for the work. Do not stop there, though; find out how much the deficiency might cost the business and how much you save in improvements. It will motivate you to reward hard work when you know how much it has saved you.

Value Recognition Over Reward

Business leaders often complain about how they cannot afford a reward and recognition program. Yet, the benefits of reduced attrition, highly engaged staff, and increased performance mean that you cannot afford to lack such a program. If your business is too small and the resources are limited, you can run a free recognition program. Focusing on recognition above rewards will save you some money.

Keep It Simple

Keeping rewards and recognition simple will give you positive outcomes. If the program is complicated, it becomes removed from the employees regardless of the value of the reward, which means that it does not drive commitment. The purpose of a recognition and reward program is to reward behaviors and work that support the business's goals, mission, and values.

Involve Staff from the Get-go

Involve staff from the early stages of developing the program. You can gather a committee to collect input from peers and ensure buy-in to the program. For example, a competition to name the program can get people excited. Encourage people to communicate with the committee and have a management representative there to guide the process to line up with business outcomes.

Reward on the Spot

The immediacy of acknowledging good performance or effort is vital. Accessible and informal rewards on the spot can be effective in driving commitment. The idea is to allow frontline agents to recognize people doing the right thing and to reward that.

Have Fun

Make recognition and reward programs part of business culture, and they will provide sparkle to the business environment, often balancing the challenges of the job.

ADDRESSING THE FACTORS THAT DRIVE INNER MOTIVATORS

William James made significant contributions to research about motivation. He theorized that behavior is driven by instinct – a species-specific pattern of behaving that is intrinsic. This theory produced controversy, with other psychologists redefining instinct. James proposed some special instincts like the urge to eat sugar or a mother's instinct to protect her baby. Later, research showed that some instinctive behaviors are learned. Another theory suggested that motivation is about maintaining homeostasis. The drive theory suggests that deviations from homeostasis are responsible for physiological needs.

Extensions to the drive theory suggest that the body aims to return to homeostasis. Whatever theory you get behind, you do not have to travel far to see that a leader can change other people's inner motivators. You can connect with the things that motivate them and their inspirations by addressing factors that drive those motivators. You discover these factors by applying empathy, as discussed in the previous chapter.

Making People Accountable

Often we describe the ideal leader as decisive, tough, and assertive. This is the appropriate approach when the situation is urgent, but a good leader needs other leadership styles in their arsenal. For example, when you have time to unpack a difficult situation and where commitment and creativity are important, you need a different style. It is unlikely that employees will perform well if they do not have ownership of their tasks.

Accountable leaders create a path for their employees to follow and hold them answerable for accomplishing a specific goal. If done well, accountability will help your team to come up with positive and measurable results. It will help your employees own what they need to do, yielding improved performance, higher satisfaction, increased belief in oneself, and more commitment to work. Accountability is accepting responsibility for the outcomes that you are expected to produce.

In being accountable, you do not blame the environment or others – there are things you can do and that you could have done to influence the outcome. People who refuse to take responsibility are victims, and no leader is a victim. Victims are passive. They accept influence. Leaders are active and always influencing an outcome. One of the core principles of accountability is viewing failure as a chance to learn. That way, you encourage people in your organization to adopt responsibility fearlessly. Your team learns to take action after a success or failure without placing blame.

Secondly, accountability is characterized by clear goals, roles, and expectations. You have to clearly define and clarify each team member's work to avoid disagreement or confusion. It keeps everyone responsible for different facets of the business. In the process, make sure that you lead by example. Create an environment that empowers employees to see outcomes as insights. Use the success to form company processes and failure as a chance to learn what to avoid. In an accountable organization, everyone influences the culture of the business, the working environment, and the business practices.

Thirdly, set milestones. There is no accountability without milestones. They help the organization stay focused, meet goals, and deliver on its competitive advantage. When milestones are hit, do not forget to celebrate them – even the tiniest gesture can go far into helping the employees overcome obstacles. While at it, develop accountable leaders. Train people in specific competencies and skills to help them understand the behaviors that demonstrate accountability. That way, leaders at all levels can deliver on commitments and see the importance of being trustworthy and reliable and can communicate their expectations, holding others accountable.

Demonstrating accountability will require that you communicate and share information. It is ensuring that people know what they need to know to handle themselves well in different situations. Communicate the importance of the outcomes so that effort is separated from the outcomes. Help your employees to own their tasks by:

Building Individual Understanding

At the beginning of any activity or initiative, ensure that people understand what you expect of them, the support and resources available, and what they need to do individually. It will help you avoid over-commitments and under-delivery. You can support understanding to help individuals be more accountable through coaching and mentorship, team meetings, and multi-rater assessments. In mentoring them, individuals see the various behaviors that demonstrate accountability. Assessments reveal to employees how their work affects others, and team meetings offer a chance for regular reviews and progress assessments.

Requiring Accountability

To ensure that your efforts yield actual results, employees need to understand why they must demonstrate accountability. Those who manage others have to clarify expectations and foster agreement and commitment to obtainable goals. As a leader, you have to insist on the delivery of the goal. You can have regular checks to review progress, provide feedback and determine the necessary support.

Individuals demonstrate their commitment daily by delivering on their expected tasks and demonstrating reliability. With the help of leaders who lead by example, coaching and training, employees can see the need for accountability and separate between results and effort, learning how to deliver both.

8

EMPOWERMENT

I f one thing has been emphasized in this book so far, it is that your leadership style is that transformational leaders know how to vary their styles with the task, team, people's knowledge and capabilities, resources, experience, and the desired results. As a leader, you make choices about what style to use in every situation. You want to involve and empower your team to enable members to give their best. This chapter explores the third aspect of being an inspirational leader – empowering your people to act.

HOW TO DELEGATE TASKS AND BUILD LEADERS?

Traditionally, leaders avoided delegating because they feared that individuals did not have the skills to complete the task at hand. Consequently, they did not grow their delegation skills. Additionally, having been inadequately prepared for their leadership role, some leaders believed that they did not have the confidence or authority to delegate. Over time, businesses started hiring people who could delegate. It was supposed that the ability to delegate is inborn, but that supposal has been refuted by recent research. Delegation is an important attribute in a leader and can be learned.

The transformational leader is the epitome of delegation. They know how to encourage others to be effective leaders. The leader knows how to get involved in the organization's goals while helping others become effective leaders. For a leader to exert such influence, there has to be a strong relationship between them and their followers because delegating also requires change. Their role is to energize those around them and build their confidence to complete their tasks. They can guide and coordinate team members to do what is needful.

Whenever possible, the transformational leader delegates. They understand the purpose of different projects and assign parts of it, helping staff members contribute the most they can, as they know the big picture. Consequently, employees are more effective. They feel that they are part of something bigger than themselves. They are sure that their work is important because they know the expectations, goals, and outcomes that they are working towards. This fosters the employee's self-image and sense of accomplishment. It saves the leader from overload and allows them to prioritize the right tasks while providing employees opportunities to learn and grow.

Research shows that leaders who delegate produce 33% more revenue. They know that they cannot do everything independently, so they task their teams to do what the leader cannot, boosting morale and improving productivity. There are many frameworks for delegating that have been proposed across time to help leaders improve their delegation skills. Of them all, the transformational leadership model is the most successful. It helps the leader foster a culture where the relationship between the leader and employees thrives. It involves shifting the values, beliefs, capabilities, and needs of the follower. The leader provides an opportunity for the follower to develop their talents and to become more proficient. If the employee shows proficiency, the leader trusts their follower's leadership skills. So, another leader is born within the department, who eventually delegates some of his responsibility to another team member.

The delegation process has a cyclic effect. The leader identifies the task they wish to delegate, and they delegate. The delegate assumes responsibility for the task and receives guidance and grooming from the leader; they communicate the task to the workplace and use the resources provided to complete the task. As they complete it, they encourage others to work on other tasks, which are measurable, and the process goes back to the beginning, where the now trained leader delegates to someone else. To delegate effectively, use the following tips:

- Clarify what you are delegating – Not all tasks have to be delegated; you have to do some things yourself. Allow others to do what does not require you to oversee.
- Delegate within their skillset – Each employee has their abilities and goals; delegate within those confines. Have the type of work you are delegating factor into your employee's career development plan.

- Define the outcomes – Giving someone work to do is not delegating. Hand projects off with the right context and connect them with the goals of the company. Let them know the resources needed to complete the task, the deadline, and the metrics for success.
- Provide resources and authority – If training is necessary to complete the task, offer it. Giving someone an impossible task only frustrates them.
- Set up clear communication channels – This will help you avoid micromanaging and provide a level of comfort for your employee to ask questions and update you on progress. Regularly check-in and provide feedback all through the project.
- Leave room for failure – The idea here is not that you think your employees will fail, but that you allow them to experiment and innovate. You demonstrate that you are open to new approaches and ideas.
- Give credit – After delegating, and observing that the work has been done well, credit it. Recognizing the success of your team will make them more engaged.

A WIZARD ENCOURAGES TEAMWORK

Everyone wins when employees work as a team. The total becomes greater than the parts because everyone covers for everyone else's negative tendencies. A highly effective team will share its workload better, develop ideas faster and create a culture that produces better results. Recent research shows that 39% of employees judge their companies as needing to improve in collaboration. This may seem like an impossible thing to achieve in a dispersed and digital workplace, but it is necessary if leaders are to build effective teams. Some people, of course, think that working in a team is slow and inefficient, but teamwork means collaboration. The leader can always speed decisions up when the need arises.

A teamwork culture in an organization will produce happier employees who feel free to share their ideas because they feel a sense of belonging. They feel valued and so, are fulfilled and productive. It fuels innovation and productivity because there is a free exchange of ideas. Eventually, teamwork allows your organization to attract and keep the top talent, serving as a bargaining chip during recruitment. Of course, having happy employees will translate to happy customers. Employees will create services and products that customers will love, which is good for your bottom line. How, then, do you encourage teamwork?

Promote Creativity

If employees collaborate, they will be positive, motivated, and creative. Encourage this by providing for group activities. You can have the team, for example, get involved in a charitable cause. Celebratory meals when the time is right also go a long way in encouraging camaraderie. When people grow comfortable, they will listen to and learn from each other and adopt new perspectives that eventually better the workplace.

Build on Individual Strengths

People become more productive when they work on something that fits their interests and strengths. Factor in each team member's expertise, strengths, and availability when assigning tasks to guarantee high-quality work. You can encourage the team to break down its responsibilities as each member knows what they can handle.

Maintain Open Communication Lines

Ineffective communication is responsible for over 80% of failure within organizations. Stay connected with your team to keep information flowing upward and downward. You can schedule regular review meetings to provide the opportunity for re-direction and feedback.

TAKE RISKS ALONGSIDE YOUR TEAM

If you are sharing goals with your team, you must also share risk. Encourage them to take risks wisely. It is easier for them to take calculated risks when they feel part of a strong team.

Empower Your Employees

Empowerment is necessary to cultivate a productive and creative team. Reward people who contribute and collaborate so that they can see the value of their efforts and ideas. Include employees in decision-making to keep them motivated and invested in the success of the organization. While at it, celebrate team achievements. Recognize major milestones and reward individual contributions.

Provide the Right Resources

Having a team with the right skills and talent is necessary, but it can mean failure if the team does not have resources. Provide a good space for meetings for your team and ensure that they have the right budget and tools to facilitate their work.

3. Provide Timely Constructive Feedback

Giving and getting feedback is necessary to improve performance. Feedback provides information that people can use to play their roles better. It motivates the employee; they no longer get by doing the bare minimum. They learn to aim higher. Well-constructed feedback encourages motivation. Even negative feedback, if handled well, can create an opportunity to learn and improve performance. It can help the employee to feel seen, appreciated, and valued. It allows them to adjust their strategies and keeps them confident and focused.

There are different types of feedback that you can use in the workplace. If they are effective, they have to be specific to an issue and have to offer a specific and actionable solution. Feedback can be negative or positive. When past behavior failed to produce the desired outcome, the feedback is negative. If the message provided helps the subject avoid future repeats of the behavior, the negative feedback is prescriptive even when the behavior was not their own.

On the other hand, positive feedback regards behavior that produced the desired outcome. It often takes the form of praise and encourages the behavior to be repeated in the future. Positive feed-forward feedback is prescriptive. These broad categories of feedback can be divided based on intent and underlying tone into:

- Appreciation – A simple positive comment can

help build a healthy relationship with an employee, but the appreciation has to be sincere. If work has been done well, mention it specifically and casually. Use names and be honest.

- Encouragement - It boosts motivation and enthusiasm. Use encouragement with new hires. Periodically check in on their learning progress and encourage them to achieve the goal.
- Personal Anecdotes – These stories create shared experiences that allow you to connect with your employees. Use your personal experiences to demonstrate that you, too, have dealt with a similar situation and to empathize.
- Guidance – When people ask questions, guide without spoon-feeding. Emphasize what you did to clarify that you are simply providing suggestions. You can combine guidance with appreciation to make it more effective.
- Forward-looking Feedback – This feedback considers the past but does not dwell on it. Focus on learning and doing better in the future. Pair it with personal anecdotes and requests for feedback on how you can make the employee's job simpler.
- Upward Feedback – Upward feedback is how

you solicit feedback from employees regarding your work. Since employees will often be uncomfortable with it, you can develop a system that ensures anonymity to hear your employee's opinions truly.

The bottom line when giving feedback is to keep it positive. Since people respond better to encouragement, guidance, and praise, you can use this to encourage the desired behavior in the future rather than dwelling on the past. Apply the following principles to give effective feedback:

Relevance

Everyone has personal and professional objectives. Feedback will be effective if it aligns with a person's goals. Develop a basic awareness of what each team member needs to be more specific with your feedback.

Focus

There are many ways to give feedback and many things you may want to say, but limit your speech only to what is necessary. Listing someone's problems can make them defensive and demoralize them. Focus on the message and set out the plan for addressing the changes you'd like to see.

Context

If you have made any linkages to arrive at your feedback, clarify them to the target. Ensure they realize how their work impacts others and what their performance contributes to the business.

Listening

You may expect to talk more since you are the one providing feedback but dial back. Rather than dominating the conversation, listen to what the other party has to say.

A TRUE WIZARD SHOWS COMPASSION

People are not machines, and your communication has to show that you know that. Your employees have a life outside of work that may sometimes affect their work. For example, your employee could have a sick child, which keeps them distracted at work. Communicate and show compassion.

Follow-up

Following up will help you see if your feedback landed. Did your employee address the issue you raised?

4. Foster Creativity, Innovation and Continuous Improvement

Continuous improvement is inevitably tied to creativity and innovation, things that move any organization forward. Leaders must focus on continuous improvement and create an environment and processes that encourage this. As a leader, it is your responsibility to create an atmosphere for new ideas to be introduced, examined, justified, and implemented into the business. You can promote new initiatives by:

Leading by Example and Demonstrating Impact

You can create regular meetings in your organization where company leaders can teach participants something they have been learning and encourage team members to reciprocate. The idea is to provide an example that others can follow. While at it, show your employees that learning and trying out new things has an impact. Fill in your team on where they fit in the society at large and the possibilities of impact that their initiatives have.

Train and Assign Demanding Tasks

No business is truly committed to continuous development if it is not committed to training employees. Set up training programs as part of the organization's culture to help people acquire the skills they need to do a particular task. Ensure that each individual has a difficult task that needs a solution outside of their comfort zone. Push them to learn on their own. To make this process run smoothly, create a checklist. That way, employees know that they are on the right track once they run through the process checklist.

Allow for Failure and Be Transparent about Difficulties

Team members thrive when they know that they can look at mistakes as opportunities to learn. Help them correct their mistakes and remove the fear of failure. Couple this with transparency about challenges. People may fail to take the initiative because they have no idea that they could add value. Let them know the obstacles the organization is facing, and they might just step up.

Allow Time for Learning

Once the team knows the challenges the company is facing, they have an opportunity to ask. Remind them of the company's goals to unify and inspire them – you may discover that team members have secret skills. If not, allow them time to learn. In addition to having a training budget, provide a learning tool and encourage employees to create time for learning and be accountable for it.

Provide Resources, Guidance, and Opportunities

Encourage your employees to explore their curiosity. It will build the mindset of a lifelong learner. Hand out rewards for those who take the initiative, even in small ways. Provide the resources for growth and praise proactive employees. Inquire about their interest in growth and provide opportunities for them to practice their new skills.

Have Regular In-person Meetings

Having regular in-person meetings can teach your team to communicate and to value their work. It can provide an opportunity for employees to grow, both professionally and personally. You can provide mentorship during those meetings and learn more about your employees.

5. Interact with Your Team to Help Them Grow

As a leader, there are different ways to interact with your team to help them grow under your wing:

- Coaching - Help employees create a broad skill set. Coaching combines teaching and advising, where you lay out a framework for the employees to follow to get to the goal. The employee directs their action plan – they can choose the path to follow. Coach when you have time to allow a learning curve.
- Teaching – Use teaching for people struggling with a specific skill. Lay out the steps the employee is to follow and explain why and how they help. When the employee knows why they need the skill, they are more motivated to learn.
- Directing – Directing specifies the steps to take to get to the goal. Be careful to direct rather than dictate. The difference is how you deliver the message. Give orders sparingly.
- Advising – You will spend a lot of time advising in your leadership. The idea is to provide clarity in a situation. When employees ask a question, for example, you are advising.

- Mentoring – Mentoring is more than offering advice. It is about becoming a colleague, role model, and guide.

Due to the importance of mentorship in transformational leadership, this section needs a bit more information. How do you become a great mentor? Proper mentorship is more than a title. The true mentor gives their energy and time to develop the skill. They embody the following qualities:

Relational Clarity

The exceptional mentor clarifies their relationship with the mentee. From the beginning, both the mentee and mentor spell out their responsibilities, goals, and roles, and what they expect of the relationship. The contract is informal, but it exists.

They Create the Time

The most important thing about mentorship is that mentors create time for their mentees. It is not always easy, but if you have decided to mentor, go all in. It communicates the value you place on the relationship.

They Champion Their Mentees Dreams

Many leaders trying to mentor others make the mistake of 'cloning versions of themselves,' but mentoring is about your protégé and helping them realize their goals. It is akin to being a parent – you help your mentee flourish and thrive in the area they venture into. Make an effort to learn about your mentee's goals and adjust your mentoring to that. You will need to listen well. Ask questions to understand your mentee better to guide them to become self-sufficient.

Model Behavior and Provide Support

After understanding your mentee, show them what they need to do to achieve their goals. If, for example, they do not know how to run a meeting, allow them to watch you as you run one. Give them the encouragement and support they need. It will accentuate their development, but be careful not to spoon-feed them. Allow space for them to figure things out on their own and when they do, praise them in public. Do not be disingenuous; only give credit when it is due.

Humbly Allow the Relationship to Grow

Great mentors admit when they do not know. They are not as concerned with the title as they are with the impact of their task. Instead, they give the relationship time to develop. Over time, the relationship becomes mutual and friendlier.

The idea is to help your employees to grow and to empower them to act. Even so, different contexts will call for different growth strategies. A leader can mentor for a while, coach when called upon, and teach when needed. The transformational leader empowers others to act by serving their needs. You coach in response to questions and to provide better outcomes, you mentor to direct specific growth within the organization, and you teach when you have skills that others do not and only as a result of coaching or mentoring.

The transformational leader must choose with intention which growth strategy to use. They recognize that it is up to them to create an atmosphere of inquiry, trust, and learning, all of which are inherent in the growth strategies. They can effortlessly switch between situations and roles in the process of improving the organization.

Empowering your people to act will mean managing your intellectual capital. It is your responsibility as a leader to understand what value your employees add to the organization. The most successful businesses invest in employee development to empower them to be their best – physically, emotionally, and intellectually. To do this, you have to learn to use the talents your people have better. You have to become a talent agent. Talent management demands that you keep an open mind and disregard outdated hiring tactics. It means that you know where to look for talent and to remove any practices that undermine efforts to boost diversity, innovation, and creativity. To better manage talent in your organization:

Plan Ahead

Often, managers ask prospective employees where they hope to be in five years in their career but hardly remember to ask themselves what their strategy for keeping talent during that period is. It is not enough to know the talent you would like. Figure out how to keep it once you have it. Do not assume that all your employees will stay – play the long game even as you execute short-term goals.

Zoom in on the Right Traits

Looking at someone's past performance is alright, but do not overrate the resume, technical expertise, and hard skills. Are your people equipped for soft skills like learnability, emotional intelligence, and drive? Consider the foundational traits that underpin knowledge acquisition.

If You Can Hire Inside, Stay Inside

Firms often hire from outside when they could find a better fit within. External hires end up taking longer and a lot of resources to adopt. They ask for higher pay than internal candidates, problems that could be solved by valuing the internal talent. If you can get someone from inside to fill a given position, pick them first – you reward commitment and loyalty, further boosting employee engagement.

Be Inclusive and Data-driven

If you hire only the people who remind you of yourself, you harm diversity and hinder team performance. Hiring people like you will deny you the benefits of complementary skill sets. Think of talent inclusively and embrace difference. Set out clear performance metrics for your current employees and make decisions based on factual data from those. Remember that the idea is not to get it right all the time but to learn and become better.

9

DISCIPLINE

People often use "discipline" and "motivation" interchangeably, but they are different things. They are not mutually exclusive, but there is a need to change how most people think about them. Motivation is the desire to do something while discipline is training by exercise and instruction. Motivation is a noun, yet discipline exists as a verb as well. Discipline is an action. Motivation can come and go. You cannot control motivation, but there is no discipline without the activity you are trying to make into a habit.

Describing someone as "disciplined" is a weak description because there is likely something they are not doing in their daily habits. It does not matter how disciplined a person is in their diet if they want to learn the piano. Learning the piano is a new habit, and it needs to be treated that way. In the same way, when trying to change something in your life, you can be inspired by motivation, but your focus should be on building disciplined habits around the new thing. It's no wonder why I tell my clients, *"Your Discipline Really Is Your Weapon,"* when mastering new leadership behaviors.

The point here is not that you do not need motivation. Motivation is often what gets you started on your new path. It is the initial nudge, but it will not keep the ball rolling uphill. Even when you are doing something you love, the daily grind can be draining. Motivation is finite. You cannot force, beg or manipulate it to stay. It causes excitement when you want to do something major, but change is complex, and the excitement will wear off. Discipline will save the day.

PEOPLE ARE HABITUAL CREATURES.

We are highly automated in the way we live. When did you last have to think about waking up and reach for your phone? There are many things you do unconsciously. The automation processes of the brain can be advantageous. You can tap into the hard wires in the process of learning discipline. In understanding how habits are established and practiced, you can figure out how to make your habits beneficial and remove the bad ones.

This means that when you start something new, you need a lot of focus. But as you do it repeatedly, you devote less and less brain activity until it becomes natural. It is the brain's way of removing the extra "fluff" to retain energy for high-performance tasks. Learning discipline takes smart practice. Simply put, motivation fires the engine, and discipline keeps it going when you are out of gas. Another implication is that to change a habit, time is a valuable resource. However big or small the thing you want to change, you need to start with small steps. The first action could be so small that it looks ridiculous, but that is the way of things. The fool is always the precursor to the hero.

When you set a low bar, there is not a huge risk attached to failure. You do not need to achieve a grand goal to feel like a success. The low bar works as an internal checkpoint because it is so simple that you feel better about yourself in achieving it. Over time, you add to the goal and keep repeating until you have a new habit. Research shows that it takes you 21 days to form a habit and 66 days to make the behavior automatic.

When setting goals, the goal is not to overwhelm yourself. In developing habits, you create discipline, and discipline succeeds where motivation fails. Without discipline, you fall for the traps of instant gratification. You forget the big picture and stop working on your long-term goals.

Before delving deeper into the idea of discipline in leadership, it is vital to talk about goals. Now that you took your time to create a vision, you need to know how to achieve it. There is interconnection between discipline and goals. For starters, discipline helps you to manage your goals effectively. It is the sustainer for motivation until you have met those goals. Discipline inspires the people you are leading to be disciplined as well. It's no wonder goal setting is vital for any transformational leader.

One of the things that contributed to the success of men like Bill Gates, Elon Musk and Steve Jobs is their mastery over setting goals that translate their vision into day-to-day work for their companies. Effective leaders set goals because goals spark and keep high-level performance in employees. You are probably familiar with the responsibilities that accompany power and the problems they bring. For example, imagine you have to navigate through a crammed professional and personal life for months, face potential burnout and make sure the company performs on all fronts. Setting goals in such a situation helps keep your focus on the critical things.

Setting goals for the leader is akin to determining where you want to get to, and if you have set those goals well, they focus and empower you to prioritize so that your world is not always a mess. You will not be frantic at the first sign of trouble because your goals give you perspective. You will not neglect your well-being and health because you know their value. Your goals always help you decide what is essential to do every day. This means that you take some time to categorize your goals by urgency and importance, then decide what you can delegate, do later or do away with.

Secondly, setting goals keeps you in charge even when motivation dwindles. Goals give you a sense of purpose for months and years. Goals help you to stay committed to doing the job. They empower you to take responsibility for your motivation and your employees' engagement. Setting compelling goals keeps you engaged in the long run and gives your business its purpose. It's no wonder that all great movements have goals. Mahatma Gandhi wanted to free India by staging non-violent resistance against British rule. Martin Luther King Jr. worked for equality for all. Because of their compelling goals for the future, these leaders were willing to give themselves to the work. They had a drive that brought change in their vision for the future.

Of course, goal setting is not always a one-time event. You often have to update and revise the goal. The point is that as you meet failures and challenges that could put you off course, goals encourage you to hold on. They constantly remind you of the big picture that you nurture to fan your passion. Yet, goal setting is not only essential for you; it helps your employees, too. It increases their efficiency and innovation. Goal-setting provides an alternative for the carrot-and-stick method many leaders use.

The transformational leader gives workers autonomy to set goals and freedom to pursue them as they deem fit. They empower workers so that as long as they deliver at deadline, they can choose where they work and have control over their process. For example, Google uses this as one of its management strategies – employees can use 20% of their working time to solve problems of their choice. Surprisingly, employees do not waste their time idling. Many of the company's new products like Google News and AdSense have been produced in the 20% free goal-setting period.

Besides creativity, ambitious goals boost morale. They encourage workers to power through challenges, and to walk into the unknown darkness with a sure resolve. Goal-setting is one of the best ways to transmit your ambition to your workers' and the public's understanding.

When I use the term "goal-setting" here, there is a specific meaning to be derived. There are different types of goals, and some work better than others because not all goals are equal. To provide a better picture of what I mean, here are three significant distinctions between goals:

Outcome vs. Behavior Goals

An outcome goal is concerned about results. A sales representative, for example, might be tasked to get 10 new clients each month, or someone on a keto diet might want to shed five pounds. To some extent, you have no control over the outcome. The sales rep might be affected by a pandemic, and the dieter could add muscle from exercising and gain weight. Of course, it is difficult to put a specific number to the impact of the external factors, but they are an undeniable influence. They often cause negative thinking that works against the goal.

On the other hand, a behavior goal zooms in on your actions. It is focused on what you do. To create a behavior goal, think of an outcome and consider what it would take to meet the goal. What is necessary to make it a reality? The actions you come up with make behavior goals. You can have both outcome and behavior goals but measure success only by the change in behavior.

Avoidance vs. Approach Goals

As the name suggests, an avoidance goal is when you do not want a negative outcome. It can set off negative thinking and reinforce what you do not want. For example, for a dieter, "avoiding junk food" could be an avoidance goal. An employee could have a goal "not to get fired." As they try to avoid junk food or not get fired, both people end up thinking more about habits that could get them to the very goal they have, which are often self-defeating.

This problem can be solved with approach goals. In an approach goal, you want to get to a positive outcome. The approach is mood-boosting. The difference between the approach and avoidance goal can seem semantic, but it makes a huge difference. An approach goal could be something like "eat healthy food" or "be excellent at work," encouraging the goal-setters to be proactive.

Abstract vs. Concrete Goals

An abstract goal does not offer much guidance when dealing with daily choices, and so it steals from motivation. Instead of having your goals as vague phrases, you can create concrete goals by being specific. To expand on the example above, you can define healthy food and what it would look like to be excellent at work. What things do you need to do to make sure you eat healthy? How much time do you need to devote to work to be excellent? Make your goals concrete and picture yourself meeting them. It makes a huge difference.

Understanding the kind of goals you are setting ensures you get the best out of goal-setting. Whether you are just starting your company, managing a small team or leading a huge organization, having the right kind of goals will give you a greater perspective, focus and motivation. It will drive the morale and efficiency of your team and help them persevere through the difficulties. Notably, there are many ways to set goals, but using the SMART system seems to be the most effective. It allows you to have a clear roadmap for getting to your intended target. It provides insight into assigning your resources so that you can move towards your goals.

SMART is an acronym for Specific, Measurable, Achievable, Relevant, and Time-based. Every element of this framework works with the rest to help you set a clear, trackable, and well-planned goal. Working with a poorly crafted goal can take away from your motivation. Here is a breakdown of the SMART framework:

S – Specific

The point here is to be as clear you can be on the goal you are targeting. The more you narrow down your goal, the easier it will be to see the necessary steps to achieving it.

M – Measurable

How will you know that you are moving towards your goal? Make sure that you highlight ways for measuring progress. Setting milestones will provide opportunities to re-evaluate and align yourself properly. It will also provide a framework for reward.

A – Achievable

Your goal needs to be reasonable to accomplish in a given timeframe. Before you start working toward your goal, figure out whether it is achievable or if there are things you need to do to prepare yourself.

R - Relevant

Are your goals relevant? Do they align with your long-term goals and values? A goal that does not lend to your objectives might not be suitable for you. Here, find out why the goal matters to you and what contribution it will make toward your long-term ambitions.

T – Time-based

How long will it take you to achieve your goal? Adding an end date will motivate you and provide a framework to prioritize. It will also give a basis for reflection. For example, if you did not achieve your goals in the set time, you can ask yourself why and make the necessary adjustments.

The SMART framework creates boundaries and highlights the necessary steps and resources to get to your goals. It shows you milestones that attest to progress and allows you to work effectively and efficiently toward your goal. It organizes the process of achieving your goals and provides a structure that can help you to begin.

Setting Leadership Goals in the Workplace

Creating and setting the goals for your leadership ensure your success and that of your team. Like your personal goals, your leadership goals should meet the SMART standards. Leadership goals are the objectives you set to improve your team's abilities, skills and overall effectiveness. They express structure and provide direction and guidance to success. Along with other duties like writing emails, preparing reports and attending meetings, goals give priority to specific aspects of leadership. They provide examples for the organization. Besides providing employees a model to emulate, leadership goals increase employee engagement, provide a sense of accomplishment and build momentum towards objectives. To set your leadership goals:

1. Identify Your Priority Goals

List all the ideas you have for goals and have a rough idea of the timeframe you need to meet them. For instance, the goals could be about a project or for the first half of the year. If you like, consult with employees. Make sure your list is expansive. From this list, make a smaller list with the most important goals. Factor in your employees' opinions because they provide insight into your team's functions. Arrange your smaller list from the most important and the one that needs to be achieved soonest.

2. Analyze Your Goals Using the SMART System

Explore your list using the SMART framework to figure out the exact goal. Make the results quantifiable and distinct. Establish how they will be achieved and set the timeframe. Move forward with the goals that pass the SMART framework.

3. Announce the Goals to Your Team

With a proper list of SMART goals, the last step is to inform your team. Make sure they understand how the new goals are to be executed. Plan to meet with your team and address any concerns or questions that might come up. Make sure to guide your team on the highest priority goals.

As a rule of thumb, make sure that all your goals are as clear as can be. People are more likely to meet clear and achievable goals. For the sake of better understanding, here is an example of a SMART goal:

To increase the productivity of my team by 20% before the end of the year.

Specificity: The objective of this goal is to increase productivity.

Measurability: It is measured by the 20% rate and can be monitored across different projects.

Attainability: It is attainable because team members need only increase their productivity by a small amount.

Relevance: It is relevant because companies measure productivity by turn-ins and due dates.

Timing: The goal has a due date.

DISCIPLINE LEADS TO SUCCESS

In another section of this chapter, we introduced the value of discipline. Discipline sets apart the mentally strong from the mentally weak. It is inseparable from success. Discipline is when you know how to say no to instant gratification and patiently work towards the big picture. It is the motor pushing you forward in life and powering you through challenges. By persevering, you are more likely to achieve the goals you have set for yourself.

At the beginning of a new year, most people make resolutions. They decide to buckle down and chase the things they have always wanted. They write them down and talk about them on social media with conviction. They start to set boundaries for themselves to help them achieve their big plans. They even make a to-do list. Over time, nothing gives. They had good intentions and great ideas but somehow seemed unable to make progress. What is the problem? What will it take to fulfill personal and professional goals?

For starters, most people do not prioritize their goals. There are two priority levels: the first one will affect your life, and the second are goals that need immediate attention. For example, getting a new job could be a level one goal. Paying an overdue bill could be a level two goal. By focusing on the outcomes, you begin to see the importance of tending to the two goal levels.

Regardless of the goal level, though, you will need discipline. When you are not diligent enough to determine what pre-selected tasks to complete, you end up giving your time to the less important ones. Without being aware of it, you steal time from your bigger plans. The transformational leader knows that there is always something to do at home and in the office. They could give their time to less important tasks and postpone achieving their goals, or they could be disciplined and work to reach the future they desire.

To forge forward, you have to change your patterns. After you have identified what goals are priorities, you must focus on them. To add incentive to your focus, you can write the consequences of missing some opportunities and the pain you will have to deal with if you do not reach your goal. As you start a project, identify who would be affected if you fail. Your subconscious will use this information to fuel you to do the job.

You will find that self-imposed deadlines are a great motivator. Not only do they work, but they also prepare you for the tasks ahead. Realizing that you will be spending yourself toward the job, your body and mind will need to be optimal. Rest and eat well before you begin a major project.

To discipline yourself, pick a time to carry out a task and think of the appointment as unbreakable. That way, you will not give room for interruptions. It is also wise to begin with the most challenging and biggest task. Stay with it until you complete it. As you do so, the other tasks will seem less daunting, and the momentum you started with will sustain you in the other tasks. Discipline is about making the necessary short-term sacrifices as you pursue long-term goals. It is about doing what you need to do, not what you want to do. A lot of research has gone into this subject. Scientists realize that willpower is inevitably tied to a good life.

One of the prevailing theories about willpower is the energy self-control model. The model postulates that the brain is like a muscle. It has limited strength that you can deplete so that no one can be disciplined all the time. The model explains lapses in self-control as having the ability to wear you out as you face another challenge. Studies show that mental exertion could compromise future discipline. While this model has had a lot of influence, not all scientists are behind it. Other scientists looking to provide a competing theory question some of its aspects.

One of the model's assertions is that exerting self-control lowers glucose levels in the blood. Some scientists doubt this assertion. They ran an experiment to test it and had volunteers fast and rest before measuring their blood glucose levels. Some volunteers were put in an environment to practice self-control while others did a task that needed little discipline. Samples were taken from all volunteers and analyzed. Scientists found that the first bunch of volunteers was less persistent in a subsequent task, but there was no drop in blood glucose levels. The results suggest that blood sugar is not connected to discipline.

Some scientists opposing the energy self-control model found that discipline is connected with motivation – the possibility of reward. Sugar does not fuel willpower, but it motivates it. All this may sound like it only works in the lab, but that is not the case. The way discipline works has many social implications. If, for example, sugar and metabolism are connected with self-control, educational institutions could stock different cafeteria foods to boost productivity in learning and optimize discipline. At work, a demotivated employee could be motivated by something as simple as a mouthwash.

WHAT DOES SELF-DISCIPLINE LOOK LIKE IN REAL LIFE?

Self-discipline is a behavior pattern where you assert willpower over your basic desires. It can be interchangeably used with self-control. It includes taking the initiative to begin and having the strength to persevere. It provides the power to withstand hardships and choose a better future over immediate satisfaction. If you are self-disciplined, you will achieve your goals because you are consistent in doing what you should.

Self-discipline also increases your self-esteem. Whenever you accomplish a goal, your brain learns that you can do whatever you set your mind to do and that builds how you view yourself. Increased self-esteem has benefits like increased respect from others. People who see you exert yourself and succeed will learn to value you. As a result, you will gain influence in other people's lives. You will have tremendous success in everything you set your mind to do, resulting in a more satisfying and rewarding life.

Conversely, if you lack self-discipline, you consistently neglect tending to your responsibilities at the right time, meaning you will not achieve your goals. There is a reason everyone who has ever been successful cultivated discipline. If you are not achieving your goals, you feel bad about yourself. You will try to justify your choices, but you will always know right from wrong. Eventually, you not only lose respect for yourself, but you also lose others' respect. This is why choosing to become disciplined could be one of the most vital decisions you will ever make. It will demand that you do what you must and quit justifying your inaction. You know you are self-disciplined when:

You know how to avoid temptation.

People always imagine that the self-disciplined person is stronger against temptation. However, self-disciplined people do not focus on lack or avoidance; they focus on managing conflicting objectives. As such, they do not grow their temptation avoidance muscle but find better ways to avoid temptation.

You are more content in life.

Studies have found links between high self-control with high life satisfaction levels. The idea that self-discipline kills excitement is untrue. When you are self-disciplined, you become more confident and better able to pursue what you want. It may take some time, but you eventually get there.

You get more of your desires, not less.

A person looking at self-discipline from outside sees someone refraining from some things, but they often fail to see what you are doing. Self-control comes from moving beyond your comfort zone. It demands deciding what you want from life and what you do not want. The undisciplined person goes through life reacting to situations, never quite deciding what they want. The self-disciplined person can assess and do what they want.

You enjoy mastering yourself.

To the onlooker, the idea of leaving a party to go jogging early seems tedious, but the self-disciplined person gains self-respect and admiration from the choice. You reap from the thrill of mastering yourself and get a lasting high that motivates you to do it some more.

You live in the moment.

A significant part of self-discipline is working towards a goal, but you are more focused on the present than most people. Being aware of the now allows you to fully live life, observe people accurately and see the impact you have on the world. It gives you more clarity in life.

You set boundaries.

The clarity you get from being in the moment allows you to set boundaries. It enables you to notice who discourages you and who pushes you forward. Since you value the goals you are working towards, you set boundaries against people who do not charge you ahead.

You know yourself.

There is a difference between reality and theory. Regardless of how much you voice your thoughts about how you respond to a situation, you never know until you are in that situation. It is the self-discipline that forces you to act. In the process, you learn who you are and what you can do.

You have more freedom.

Not many people know this, but self-discipline is a type of freedom. It is freedom from other people's demands and expectations, laziness, fear and weakness. It allows you to experience your inner strength and master your gifts. As you practice self-discipline, you begin to see how your addictions, bad habits and culture control you, and you begin to take more control over how you live.

You are better at pursuing long-term objectives.

Successful people are self-disciplined. They have long learned the value of going the extra mile to get what they want. They know how to make little promises to themselves and fulfill them. The benefit is that the more commitments you meet, the better you feel and the higher you go.

Self-discipline does not take away from having fun. You can enjoy life more because you do not feel guilt from the things you know you should have done that you did not do. You are aware that you tended to your priorities, so you relax without nagging feelings. As you build discipline, you put more weight on what you do than on your intellect. True, intelligence has many advantages, but it is discipline that takes you far. Because you are self-disciplined, you practice the things that matter. Knowing that the more you do them, the better you become eventually, makes having self-discipline easier.

How do you master self-discipline?

Studies show that self-control is tied to happiness and greater financial security. It is a better academic performance predictor than IQ. It is also self-discipline that has the most significant contribution to relationships, diet and nutrition. It keeps people employed. The good news is that you are not destined for mediocrity if self-discipline does not come naturally to you. You can learn it by:

Avoiding Temptation

Not having to use self-control is the best way to be good at it. People have limited willpower, and you do not want to use yours all day. Save it for unexpected situations.

Rising to the Occasion

Some people see discipline as abundance and others as scarcity. Whichever camp you are in, it is a self-fulfilling prophecy. Your best bet is to see discipline as abundance so that you can know how to regulate yourself and be your best version. It will mean deploying energy in a sustained fashion.

Practicing Self-care

Sleep deprivation impairs self-control. To be disciplined, get enough sleep. That way, you will be healthier in the long term because you are not managing acute stress.

Breaking Goals into Small Parts

Whether you are working to meet a deadline or are training for a marathon, you need to have mini-milestones to be disciplined. Setting small goals will make you feel happier and motivated. Imagine you are driving towards a mountain. As some miles pass, the mountain does not seem closer, but you can see progress when you look through the window. Small goals are like that. They give you a perception of movement towards your goals.

Following Through

When a self-disciplined person is ready for change, they get proactive about making it happen. If they seek advice, they run with it. It is the person without self-discipline who needs a lot of hand-holding.

Bear in mind that self-discipline is key to perseverance. Success is daily acts of discipline, and you build that discipline up like you build muscle. You will meet many obstacles on the way, but when you face them and overcome them, you develop perseverance which can be thought of as active self-discipline. You might find it helpful to calendar important days and write down what you gain from self-discipline because nothing in the world can replace persistence – not talent, not genius and certainly not education.

SELF-DISCIPLINE BEGINS WITH KNOWING YOUR PURPOSE

We began the chapter by exploring the symbiosis between discipline and motivation. To recap, motivation draws from an innate drive to do something, and it does not last forever. It is a temporary boost by your brain to set you in the right direction. On the other hand, discipline is the ability to keep walking in the right direction long after motivation has waned. It is far more important than motivation. In another sense, discipline is "what you do" and motivation is "why you do." The self-disciplined person has learned self-control so that they are not a slave to their motivations.

It is the discipline that shapes your feeling, thinking and actions to adopt a new behavior. It serves you when motivation urges you to do something else. With self-discipline, you can regulate your behavior towards improvement. It is based on reason and thinking so that it helps you self-correct when you veer off a path. Where the undisciplined is a slave to their passions, appetites and moods, discipline enables you to choose what is suitable for the long term.

To get the best results, let motivation work alongside discipline. Motivation could be what initially inspires you, and self-discipline becomes what keeps you going. To make all these less theoretical, here are some things you can do:

- Clarify the right thing to do. You cannot self-discipline if you have no idea what would be right for you.
- Consider motivation to be input. What does your body want? What about your mind and emotions? Factor these in.
- Decide from the get-go. Decide how you will behave beforehand. That way, it will be easier to respond well when you are in the thick of things.
- Check in with yourself. Make it a habit to ask yourself what you want to do and what the right thing is. Sometimes, they will not be the same thing.
- Use motivation to better yourself. Motivation can fuel your discipline. Shape your thinking and feelings progressively until you form a

habit. Link your actions to good feelings so that it will be easy to see the reward for your efforts and choices.

Discipline and motivation can become contagious, but it is essential to talk about cultivating consistent motivation. If self-discipline and motivation are to work together and motivation often wanes, what do you do when you are demotivated? It is common to find yourself in a motivational slump. Sometimes, it even goes on for a period. In such situations, there are a few things you need as much as the right attitude. Armed with a good attitude, you can implement the following steps to self-motivate:

1. Start small. Keep things that motivate you close. Use them as triggers to remind yourself to keep going.
2. Watch who you spend time with. Regularly meet with positive and motivated people. This could be something as small as having a conversation with someone who likes to share ideas. Motivated people will help you see opportunities and to grow.
3. Never stop learning. Try to take in all that you can. The more you know, the more confident you will be in beginning projects.

4. See the silver lining. When dealing with a challenge, get in the habit of finding what is good in the challenge.
5. Quit thinking. When an action is called for, take it. Rather than dwelling on countless analyses, get started and you will develop momentum.
6. Know who you are. Ensure you note the things that motivate you. Once you recognize your patterns, you can work to develop them.
7. Track progress. Regularly document how your projects are going. When you see growth, you will want to nurture the projects.
8. Help other people. In seeing others do well, you will be motivated to pursue success.

As you work on staying motivated, you may want to consider stoicism and the things you can learn from it. Stoicism is a philosophy founded in Athens and is hinged on wisdom, temperance, justice and courage. It postulates that happiness is based on behavior. The philosophy reminds us of the unpredictability in the world, the brevity of life and the value of self-control. The root of the philosophy is taking any obstacles you meet and using them to your advantage. The philosophy has much to say about self-discipline.

First, self-discipline begins with knowing your purpose. Stoics believe that everyone has a purpose, and we must understand it and pursue it. It provides for us a "why" which drives all activities we do. The point? If you want to do something, do it. Practice something because you want to. Self-discipline is finding compelling reasons to pursue something and committing to them.

Stoicism also teaches about quenching your appetites. After you have a purpose, you need a plan for accomplishing your goal. You can then commit to the actions you need to take in the pursuit of that goal. Self-discipline then becomes the ability to do what you have to do no matter how you feel. Everything you want out of life depends on doing the necessary actions to achieve it. Having small achievable goals will help you work toward your desire in small steps and avoid succumbing to your appetites that would otherwise sidetrack you.

Thirdly, self-discipline is connected with showing up daily. With a definite purpose and a good plan, most people still fail because they are not consistent. Showing up daily and doing the needful is part of the process. You have to put in many hours of work to benefit, and self-discipline becomes consistency. It is finding the desire to repeat something until you reap the benefits. Roman Emperor Marcus Aurelius advocated for disciplining yourself in small things to make progress. You can build self-discipline by facing hardship voluntarily. Make your life uncomfortable in some way to develop the strength to stay the course.

Another thing the stoic philosophy advocates for is control over your mind. You cannot control external factors. You can only control how you respond. As such, small things do not need to bother you. Staying in control over your mind will keep you from being derailed. Remind yourself of what is yours to control and embrace what you cannot. If you learn this, then you will never play the victim. You do your job without complaining or making excuses. You assume responsibility and teach yourself to avoid self-pity. It is a sign of mental strength to resist the urge to pawn off blame. Victimizing yourself means you give up control and the resolve to change.

According to the philosophy, self-discipline cannot be divorced from delayed gratification. Delayed gratification is about waiting before you get what you desire. It is resisting temptation and sticking to your goals to get something better in the future. When other people dislike you, you will realize that you do not need to be anxious about it. Naysayers just love to oppose, and taking in their opinion will hinder your self-discipline. You can, instead, find people who are wise in a given area and emulate them. Model your life after someone of good character. Ask yourself what they would do in your situation and do that. Their experience can help you to become more disciplined.

Perhaps the most important thing you can learn from stoicism regarding self-discipline is reviewing your day. One way to make sure you become disciplined is to examine yourself and identify areas where you are weak. Doing this regularly will help you become self-aware. Ask yourself the things you are doing well and what you need to improve on. Forgive yourself when you mess up and find ways to do better the next time. Self-discipline starts with mastering your thoughts, which is why you should also guard against myths regarding self-discipline. The most common myths include:

1. If you have no discipline, you will be lazy and without direction.

Self-discipline is necessary, but it can be a crutch. Constantly forcing yourself to do things you would rather not do may not be the best approach. Instead of focusing on what you dread, focus on the end goal and motivate yourself to work. Magnifying your desire will influence your actions and give you a positive mindset. Self-discipline becomes, and rightfully so, a supplementary tool.

2. Self-discipline is the only path to success.

When you break it down, self-discipline will not take you anywhere if your goals are not well-defined. More significant than having a rigid concept of self-discipline is knowing the things you are trying to do. For example, you can discipline yourself to be up at 4 am but spend the whole day tired and unable to do anything constructive.

3. Self-discipline is difficult.

It may be hard to discipline yourself sometimes, but it is more difficult living without discipline. For example, if you eat junk food too often, you will have to handle the consequences in the long term. It becomes harder to live without discipline than to discipline yourself.

4. Willpower and discipline are the same.

Discipline is about developing healthy habits while willpower is being conscious of how you behave. Resolve will allow you to say no to pizza when you are on a diet, but self-discipline will help you accept that you do not need pizza, so you stock your refrigerator with vegetables.

5. Self-discipline is always staying in control.

It is not true what most people assume: that the more discipline you have, the more control you will have. Self-discipline is controlling yourself and your actions, never your surroundings.

6. Self-discipline is removed from emotion.

Being human is having emotion. No matter how disciplined you become, you will still feel. Self-discipline needs to be supplemented with emotional awareness. There may be times you need to take a timeout to connect with your emotions and avoid projecting them onto others.

7. Self-discipline is about not doing what you want.

A self-disciplined life is not a constricted and narrow life. It is a life where rather than constantly reacting to things, you have set up habits that empower you to choose things that support what you want. It helps you have a life full of positive situations, rewarding connections and supportive friendships.

The good thing is that you can train your brain to be more disciplined. The human brain has a network that regulates many behavioral functions and underlies many skills, including regulating emotions. You can train the network to be better at control and learn to reduce maladaptive behaviors with a bit of exertion. This training is necessary because your mindset and your approach to discipline are everything at the end of the day. Such training enables you to think abundantly and positively with no room for failure manifesting the things you want out of life. Yet, discipline comes easier if you love what you do, but sometimes that is not possible. You must remember that you need to be patient.

Many people know that patience is a virtue, but few ever learn how to be patient. Like other skills, the more patience you practice, the more patient you become. Patience is necessary for how you relate with employees, communication, business negotiation and achieving your goals. Patience gives you many benefits, including:

1. Positive rewards. When you are patient, you can delay gratification. You can work towards your goals in a dedicated effort. Patience rewards you with positive rewards like increased customer satisfaction, more sales, and stronger profits.
2. Better decision-making. Patience is one of the most important resources in decision-making. When you are patient, you are mindful enough to focus on the moment, making better choices.

3. Positive reputation. Successful businessmen stand out through patience. It is patience that gives you grit and creates an excellent reputation.
4. Self-possession. Patience allows you to control yourself. You give yourself the time you need to respond to an event instead of following your emotions.
5. Tolerance. Patience makes you tolerant. It gives you the foresight to expect challenges and deal with them with courage and optimism.
6. Hope. Patience births hope, which makes you willing to keep trying.
7. Good workplace culture. Patient devotion creates a culture of engagement that paves the way to success. It increases your opportunities for being where you want to be, helps you treat others well and increases the possibility of kindness from others in response.
8. Excellence. Talent can be described as patience that has been earned over a long period. You become better and ultimately fulfill your potential with patience.

THE THREE TRAPS OF LEADERSHIP

Even though discipline is your weapon, there are things that you need to watch out for. Often, a leader's weaknesses are exposed after falling into one or two of the following traps.

1. The Loss of Vision

When a leader loses their vision, they lose sight of their responsibility to their team. You begin to make choices that are not aligned with where you want to be. If you are not vigilant, you can fall into this trap and lose your hard work. The more successful you become, the more you have to check your heart to see whether you are on the right track. As a leader, it is your job to bear the vision for your company. If you lose your vision, employees will too. You and your employees become unrestrained, walking in the darkness without signposts or boundaries.

2. Isolation

It is not uncommon for successful people to become isolated. Isolation often starts when some relationships are sacrificed for dedication and hard work. As you gain more influence, people begin to choose their words around you and authentic relationships become fewer. The leader-follower relationship in a business, if not mitigated, can cause you to be even more isolated. When you control a person's income and time, it creates a wall in the relationship. You have a responsibility to humble yourself to seek transparency and authenticity with your communication.

3. False Sense of Control

As you become successful, you could lose sight of your journey and forget all the people who helped you get there. The realization that your actions have influence gives you a sense of control. You find yourself constantly wanting to conquer the future as if you could do it alone. A sense of power is the ultimate test of humility.

CONCLUSION

Chess is a recreational and competitive board game played between two players. Today, chess is one of the world's most popular games, played by millions of people worldwide. It is a game that has striking similarities to the magic of leadership. Chess is a game of strategies and knowledge; the player needs to play by the rules of the game, apply strategies, and show emotional endurance in time.

Both players have the same opportunities; the game is played on a board with 64 squares arranged in an eight-by-eight grid. At the start, one player controls the white pieces, while the other takes the black ones. Each player controls 16 pieces: a king, a queen, two rooks, two knights, two bishops and eight pawns. The object of the game is to checkmate the opponent's king.

Just like chess, your leadership journey is not linear, you need to be a wizard to add the magic and unlock your own potential. Sometimes, you must move in different directions and play different roles. The magic is in how you embrace your superpowers. They may be negotiating strategically, leading people with empathy and respect. Whatever your superpowers are, use them. If going through the book you've discovered some that were lacking, it is my hope that you used the principles given to upgrade them.

Experts agree that Oprah Winfrey is an example of leadership that everyone should emulate. Her ability to inspire her team and to carry out her vision while maintaining mass appeal is unparalleled. How does she do it? This book has deconstructed her leadership technique. It has demonstrated that her platform is built on many factors, which you can learn. She did not start as she is, but she learned how to grow her team based on her vision and values and rose from nothing into a renowned businesswoman in over 30 years.

Her leadership style, transformational leadership, inspires positive changes in those who follow. Transformational leaders are passionate, enthusiastic, and energetic. They are concerned about the process and involved, looking to help every group member succeed. They encourage the motivation of their followers and exemplify moral standards in their organization, encouraging others to do the same. The transformational leader builds a company culture by encouraging employees to work for the common good. They foster an ethical workplace with clear priorities, standards, and values and emphasize cooperation, open communication, and authenticity.

Transformational leaders provide mentoring and coaching while allowing their employees to make their choices and own their responsibility. Simply put, they stimulate and inspire their followers to achieve the extraordinary while developing themselves in the process. They help others to become leaders by responding to individual needs, empowering them, and aligning their goals and objectives to those of the group and the larger organization.

From this book, you have been introduced to the nine dimensions of transformational leadership and explored what influence looks like in leadership. You know why you need a vision, how to create a compelling vision and how to get your team behind it. You can harness the power of discipline and transformative communication. You know that challenges do not have to knock you out; you can master them and inspire others to do the same through empathy. You can get your followers to commit to change and empower them to act. You know exactly what it looks like to be an inspirational leader. You have actionable steps to transform your leadership style into a style that will give the best results for you and your team. The ball is now on your court. Go ahead, achieve the impossible!

While at it, take someone with you by letting them know what you loved about this book on Amazon.

Dear Reader,

I hope you like it!

As a self-publishing author, I rely on readers like you to help promote my work and serve humanity better by doing my best to write, share, coach and train the next generation of leaders like you.

Please, consider posting an online review on Amazon, a short review, audio, or a picture highlighting the page you enjoyed the most. Book reviews are essential to any book. They help potential buyers make confident decisions when getting and buying books.

www.amazon.com/review/create-review/
asin=B0976GLTRF/

Unlock the leader in you.

Your coach, Marlene Gonzalez.

ABOUT THE AUTHOR

Marlene Gonzalez is the founder and the president of Life coaching group LLC. focusing on Leadership development and executive coaching. She passionately pursues one vision- "To advance, develop and promote minority leaders." She is a renowned executive coach and facilitator. She is the author of the coaching series Leadership Wizard; "Number 1 New Release book in the Education and Leadership category". Her book series specializes in transformational leadership topics such as:

- *Leadership Wizard. The Nine Dimensions. Unlock the Leader in You. The Discipline of Coaching Yourself to Fearlessly Lead, Influence, Inspire and Empower Others.*
- *Assertive Wizard. How To Boost Confidence, Get Your Message Across, And Speak With Impact.*
- *Change Wizard. Master The Art Of Leading Change And Working Together for a Common Purpose.*

- *Confident Wizard.* Turn Self Doubt Into Confidence: The Ultimate Guide To Lead With Authenticity, Purpose, and Resilience.

Once you master these and many other topics she covers, you can transform your life and become a more successful leader. In addition, you will find that her books have a straight-to-the-point approach and easy to implement actions. She is passionate about sharing her insights and resources on transformational leadership through a combination of Insights Discovery, the psychology of C. G. Jung, her corporate career experience and her professional coaching expertise.

González held many executive corporate positions in the US, Europe, and Latin America. She is the former Senior Director of Global Training, Learning, and Development for McDonald's Corporation. Marlene holds a BS, an Executive MBA/PAG, and a graduate diploma on managerial Issues in the global enterprise from Thunderbird University. www. marlenegonzalez.com

REFERENCES

What is a pawn promotion? https://www.chess.-com/terms/pawn-promotion#what-is-pawn-promotion

10 healthy ways to bounce back from failure. (n.d.). Verywell Mind. https://www.verywellmind.com/healthy-ways-to-cope-with-failure-4163968

15 ways leaders can encourage employees to take initiative. (2020, June 11). Small Business Trends. https://smallbiztrends.com/2020/06/15-ways-leaders-can-encourage-employees-to-take-initiative.html

4 steps to recovering from making a major mistake at work. (2018, May 16). Inc.com. https://www.inc.com/john-discala/4-ways-to-bounce-back-after-making-a-mistake-at-work.html

The 6 types of basic emotions and their effect on human behavior. (n.d.). Verywell Mind. https://www.verywellmind.com/an-overview-of-the-types-of-emotions-4163976

The 6 types of basic emotions and their effect on human behavior. (n.d.). Verywell Mind. https://www.verywellmind.com/an-overview-of-the-types-of-emotions-4163976

6 ways truly effective leaders deliver feedback. (2018, February 13). Inc.com. https://www.inc.com/glenn-leibowitz/6-ways-truly-effective-leaders-deliver-feedback.html

7 mistakes employees make and how to deal with them. (n.d.). The Balance Careers. https://www.thebalancecareers.com/how-to-resolve-employee-mistakes-4129670

7 proven ways to encourage teamwork in the workplace. (2019, May 29). Igloo Software. https://www.igloosoftware.com/blog/teamwork-in-the-workplace/

7 tips about how to delegate tasks to your team. (n.d.). The Balance Careers. https://www.thebalancecareers.com/delegation-as-a-leadership-style-1916731

Oprah Winfrey - Leadership style & principles | Geeknack. (2020, November 28). Geeknack. https://www.

geeknack.com/2020/11/27/oprah-winfrey-leadership-style-and-principles/

Accountability in leadership: 6 skills all leaders should master. (2020, November 20). Notre Dame. https://www.notredameonline.com/resources/leadership-and-management/6-skills-for-leadership-accountability/

Advance Nursing Institute. (n.d.). *The Cycle of Leadership through Transformational Delegation Model in Healthcare.* Advance Nursing Institute (ANI). https://advancenursing.net/uploads/courses/58/the%20cycle%20of%20leadership%20through%20transformational%20delegation%20model%20in%20a%20health%20care%20organization.pdf

Are you empathic? 3 types of empathy and what they mean. (2011, August 3). Psychology Today. https://www.psychologytoday.com/us/blog/cutting-edge-leadership/201108/are-you-empathic-3-types-empathy-and-what-they-mean

Becoming a great mentor. (n.d.). https://www.apa.org. https://www.apa.org/monitor/2019/01/cover-mentor

Carreau, D., & Contributor. (2019, July 15). *Here's exactly what to do—and say—after you've made a mistake at work.* CNBC. https://www.cnbc.com/2019/07/15/heres-exactly-what-to-doand-sayafter-youve-made-a-mistake-at-work.html

Charney, C. (2006). *The leader's tool kit: Hundreds of tips and techniques for developing the skills you need.* Amacom Books.

Cornett, I. (n.d.). *5 ways to demonstrate leadership accountability & ensure it in others.* Experiential Organizational Training & Development | Eagle's Flight. https://www.eaglesflight.com/blog/5-ways-to-demonstrate-leadership-accountability-ensure-it-in-others

Create a positive pandemic as an emotional contagion. (2020, July 23). Nina Amir. https://ninaamir.com/positive-pandemic-emotional-contagion/

Developing empathy: 8 strategies & worksheets to become more empathic. (2020, September 16). PositivePsychology.com. https://positivepsychology.com/empathy-worksheets/

Emotional contagion: The social power of emotions explained. (2021, February 9). PositivePsychology.com. https://positivepsychology.com/emotional-contagion/

Emotional disposition. (n.d.). SpringerLink. https://link.springer.com/referenceworkentry/10.1007/978-3-319-16999-6_3052-1

Emotions. Emotional dispositions. (n.d.). ChestofBooks.com: Read Books Online for Free.

https://chestofbooks.com/health/psychology/G-F-Stout/A-Manual-Of-Psychology/Emotions-Emotional-Dispositions.html

Empathetic leadership. (2018, September 27). Exploring your mind. https://exploringyourmind.com/empathetic-leadership/

Entrepreneurial motivating factors: Internal and external factors. (2014, May 20). Your Article Library. https://www.yourarticlelibrary.com/entrepreneurship/motivation-entrepreneurship/entrepreneurial-motivating-factors-internal-and-external-factors/40682

(n.d.). Forbes. https://www.forbes.com/sites/ashiraprossack1/2018/07/31/these-6-communication-styles-should-be-in-every-leaders-toolbox/?sh=3841fac35fd7

(n.d.). Forbes. https://www.forbes.com/sites/forbescoachescouncil/2019/06/19/do-you-know-when-to-coach-teach-train-or-mentor/?sh=55543dfc4f69

(n.d.). Forbes. https://www.forbes.com/sites/jennagoudreau/2010/10/22/how-to-lead-like-oprah-winfrey-own-rachael-ray-dr-oz-phil/?sh=333d37395582 (n.d.). Forbes. https://www.forbes.com/sites/ melodywilding/2019/08/05/8-habits-of-highly-empathetic-leaders/?sh=725f59ce6de7

How do transformational leaders inspire and motivate followers? (n.d.). Verywell Mind. https://www. verywellmind.com/what-is-transformational-leadership-2795313

How the best managers identify and develop talent. (2020, January 9). Harvard Business Review. https://hbr.org/ 2020/01/how-the-best-managers-identify-and-develop-talent

How to be an empathetic leader - Lolly Daskal | Leadership. (2018, April 9). Lolly Daskal. https://www.lollydaskal. com/leadership/how-to-be-an-empathetic-leader/

How to delegate effectively: 7 tips for managers. (2020, January 14). Business Insights - Blog. https://online. hbs.edu/blog/post/how-to-delegate-effectively

The importance of self-confidence in leadership. (2020, November 17). SmallBusinessify.com. https:// smallbusinessify.com/the-importance-of-self-confidence-in-leadership/

Inspirational leadership traits: Oprah. (2015, July 4). The CORE. https://collegeofrealestate.net/ 201573inspirational-leadership-traits-oprah/

Learning, E. I. (2019, September 23). *Why is giving and receiving feedback important?* Engage in Learning. https://engageinlearning.com/blog/why-is-giving-and-receiving-feedback-important/

Masterful leaders – The leader as coach, mentor and teacher. (2019, August 29). gothamCulture. https://gothamculture.com/2019/04/11/masterful-leaders-the-leader-coach-mentor-teacher/

Misconceptions about values. (2014, January 16). Joshua Spodek. https://joshuaspodek.com/misconceptions-about-values

Motivation | Introduction to psychology. (n.d.). Lumen Learning – Simple Book Production. https://courses.lumenlearning.com/wmopen-psychology/chapter/introduction-motivation/

Patterson, J. (n.d.). *The core principles of leadership accountability.* KnowledgeWave: Microsoft Office 365 Training Experts. https://www.knowledgewave.com/blog/leadership-accountability-principles

Principles of an effective reward and recognition program. (2015, September 30). Contact Center Pipeline. https://www.contactcenterpipeline.com/Article/principles-of-an-effective-reward-and-recognition-program

Transformational leadership theory - Meaning, criticisms and its implications. (n.d.). Management Study Guide - Courses for Students, Professionals & Faculty Members. https://managementstudyguide.com/transformational-leadership.htm

Types of feedback: Everything you need to know. (2019, July 30). UpRaise. https://upraise.io/blog/types-of-feedback/

Understanding emotional contagion in leadership. (n.d.). Specialist Recruitment Agency in Dublin - Next Generation. https://www.nextgeneration.ie/blog/2016/01/understanding-emotional-contagion-in-leadership

Understanding others' value and their values. (2012, December 29). Joshua Spodek. https://joshuaspodek.com/understanding-values

Understanding the values of others. (2017, October 25). The Pacific Institute®. https://thepacificinstitute.com/blog/2017/10/25/understanding-the-values-of-others/

What are the big 5 personality traits? (n.d.). Verywell Mind. https://www.verywellmind.com/the-big-five-personality-dimensions-2795422

What is value? What are values? (short version). (2014, January 16). Joshua Spodek. https://joshuaspodek.com/values-short-version

White, S. K. (n.d.). *What is transformational leadership? A model for sparking innovation.* CIO. https://www.cio.com/article/3257184/what-is-transformational-leadership-a-model-for-motivating-innovation.html

Whitmore, J. (n.d.). *5 ways to lead by example at work.* Entrepreneur. https://www.entrepreneur.com/article/238171

Why great leaders (Like Richard Branson) inspire instead of motivate. (2017, March 30). Inc.com. https://www.inc.com/marissa-levin/why-great-leaders-like-richard-branson-inspire-instead-of-motivate.html

Why leaders need to understand people's motivations. (2021, February 8). Full Potential Group. https://fullpotentialgroup.com/3-reasons-why-leaders-need-to-understand-peoples-motivations/

Your INTJ personality type and your Enneagram type. (2020, August 17). Psychology Junkie. https://www.psychologyjunkie.com/2020/02/28/your-intj-personality-type-and-your-enneagram-type/

Your response to mistakes defines you. (2019, November 9). Farnam Street. https://fs.blog/2014/09/mistakes/